REA's Interactive Flashcards™

U.S. HISTORY
1912 - Present

**Staff of Research and Education Association,
Dr. M. Fogiel, Director**

 Research & Education Association
61 Ethel Road West
Piscataway, New Jersey 08854

REA's INTERACTIVE FLASHCARDS™
UNITED STATES HISTORY 1912 - PRESENT

Copyright © 1999 by Research & Education Association. All rights reserved. No part of this book may be reproduced in any form without permission of the publisher.

Printed in the United States of America

Library of Congress Catalog Card Number 98-67215

International Standard Book Number 0-87891-166-9

Research & Education Association, Piscataway, New Jersey 08854

REA's Interactive Flashcards
What they're for
How to use them

They come in a book, not in a box of hundreds of loose cards.

They are most useful as test time approaches to help you check your test readiness.

They are a good tool for self-study and also for group study. They can even be used as a competitive game to see who scores best.

They work with any text.

The interactive feature is a unique learning tool. With it, you can write in your own answer to each question which you can then check against the correct answer provided on the flip side of each card.

You will find that the flashcards in a book have several advantages over flashcards in a box.

You don't have to cope with hundreds of loose cards. Whenever you want to study, you don't have to decide beforehand which cards you are likely to need; you don't have to pull them out of a box (and later return them in their proper place). You can just open the book and get going without ado.

A very detailed index will guide you to whatever topics you want to cover.

A number of blank card pages is included, in case you want to construct some of your own Q's and A's.

You can take along REA's flashcard book anywhere, ready for use when you are. You don't need to tote along the box or a bunch of loose cards.

REA's Flashcard books have been carefully put together with REA's customary concern for quality. We believe you will find them an excellent review and study tool.

Dr. M. Fogiel
Program Director

P.S. As you could tell, you could see all the flashcards in the book while you were in the store; they aren't sealed in shrink-wrap.

Questions

Q1

What explains the increased popularity of the Socialist party in the election of 1912?

*Your Own Answer*_____

Q2

Who were the main contestants for the Republican nomination in 1912?
a) Who won the nomination?
b) How did this nomination process affect the general election?

*Your Own Answer*_____

Q3

a) In the election of 1912, what was the term used to describe Democratic nominee Woodrow Wilson's platform?
b) What were two features of this platform?

*Your Own Answer*_____

Correct Answers

A1

The division among both Republicans and Democrats into conservative and progressive factions

A2

Incumbent President William Howard Taft and former President Theodore Roosevelt were the contestants.
a) Taft won the nomination
b) Roosevelt and many of his supporters bolted the Republican Party to form the Progressive or Bull Moose Party.

A3

a) Wilson's platform was called the New Freedom.
b) Two features of the platform were to restore economic competition through the breakup of monopolies and lower tariffs.

Questions

Q4

There were four main contestants in the 1912 election. Name the order of finish.

Your Own Answer_____

Q5

Woodrow Wilson was governor of what state before becoming president?

Your Own Answer_____

Q6

The Sixteenth Amendment to the Constitution was ratified in February of 1913. What did this amendment do?

Your Own Answer_____

Correct Answers

A4

1) Woodrow Wilson
2) Theodore Roosevelt
3) William Howard Taft
4) Eugene Debs

A5

New Jersey

A6

It authorized the income tax.

Questions

Q7

When was the Federal Reserve Act passed?
a) What was the purpose of creating a new currency called Federal Reserve Notes?
b) What mechanism was created to supervise the Federal Reserve system?

*Your Own Answer*_____

Q8

The Clayton Antitrust Act of 1914 was intended to supplement an existing piece of legislation.
a) What was the name of the legislation?
b) How did the Clayton Act affect the organization of corporations?

*Your Own Answer*_____

Q9

What did the Federal Trade Commission Act of 1914 do?

*Your Own Answer*_____

Correct Answers

A7

The Federal Reserve Act was passed in 1913.
a) The currency was designed to expand and contract with the volume of business activity and borrowing.
b) The Federal Reserve Board was created to supervise the system.

A8

a) The existing piece of legislation was the Sherman Antitrust Act.
b) Stock ownership by a corporation in a competing corporation was prohibited, and interlocking directorates of competing corporations were prohibited.

A9

The law prohibited all unfair trade practices without defining them, and created a commission of five members appointed by the president. The commission was empowered to issue, cease, and desist orders to corporation, to stop actions considered to be in restraint of trade, and to bring suit in courts if the orders were not obeyed.

Questions

Q10

Which president appointed Louis Brandeis to the Supreme Court?

Your Own Answer

Q11

What did the Federal Farm Loan Act of 1916 do?

Your Own Answer

Q12

What did the Child Labor Act of 1916 do?
a) Why was the law especially significant?
b) What happened to the law in 1918?

Your Own Answer

Correct Answers

A10

President Wilson

A11

The law divided the country into twelve regions and established a Federal Land Bank in each region. The banks made farm mortgage loans at reasonable interest rates.

A12

It forbade shipment in interstate commerce of products whose production had involved the labor of children under 14 or 16, depending on the product. a) The law was especially significant because it was the first time that Congress regulated labor within a state using the interstate commerce power. b) The law was declared unconstitutional by the Supreme Court in 1918 on the grounds that it interfered with the powers of the states.

Questions

Q13

What was the impact of the Kerr-McGillicuddy Act of 1916?

*Your Own Answer*_____

Q14

Who did the Democrats and Republicans nominate for president in 1916?

*Your Own Answer*_____

Q15

In the election of 1916, Woodrow Wilson increased his popular vote by almost 50% from 1912. Why?

*Your Own Answer*_____

Correct Answers

A13

This law initiated a program of workmen's compensation for federal employees.

A14

The Democrats nominated Woodrow Wilson and the Republicans nominated Charles Evans, an associate justice of the Supreme Court.

A15

Most of his additional votes came from people who had voted for the Progressive or Socialist tickets in 1912.

Questions

Q16

What was the basic promise of Wilson's "New Freedom" foreign policy?

*Your Own Answer*_____

Q17

What were the Conciliation Treaties, and what did they illustrate?

*Your Own Answer*_____

Q18

By what action did Wilson signal his repudiation of dollar diplomacy?

*Your Own Answer*_____

Correct Answers

A16

Wilson promised a more moral foreign policy, denounced imperialism and dollar diplomacy, and advocated the advancement of democratic capitalist governments throughout the world.

A17

Secretary Bryan negotiated treaties with 29 nations under which they agreed to submit disputes to international commissions for conciliation not arbitration. While the treaties probably had no practical effect, they illustrated idealism of the administration.

A18

He withdrew American involvement from the six-power loan consortium of China.

Questions

Q19

In 1912, President Wilson sent American marines to Nicaragua to maintain order. What treaty resulted from this intervention?

Your Own Answer

Q20

What event precipitated the American military intervention in Mexico in 1916?

Your Own Answer

Q21

What was the Submarine Crisis of 1915?

Your Own Answer

Correct Answers

A19

The intervention resulted in the Bryan-Chamosso Treaty of 1914, which gave the United States an option to build a canal through the country.

A20

Former Mexican general Francisco "Pancho" Villa shot 16 Americans on a train in northern Mexico and burned the border town of Columbus, New Mexico. Villa was actually hoping to provoke American intervention as a means of undermining his political rival Venustiano Carranza.

A21

The Germans sank the British liner *Lusitania* off the coast of Ireland on May 7, 1915, resulting in the loss of 1,198 lives, including 128 Americans. President Wilson had argued that Americans had a right as neutrals to travel safely on such ships, and he strongly protested the German action.

Questions

Q22

What was the Sussex Pledge?

*Your Own Answer*_____

Q23

How did World War I affect the 1916 presidential election?

*Your Own Answer*_____

Q24

What two events contributed to the American declaration of war against Germany?

*Your Own Answer*_____

Correct Answers

A22

The Germans pledged to cease all surprise submarine attacks on all shipping, whether belligerent or neutral, armed or unarmed after torpedoing but not sinking the unarmed French channel steamer *Sussex* on March 24, 1916.

A23

The slogan, "He kept us out of the war" became the principal theme of Democratic campaign materials, and it apparently contributed to Wilson's victory.

A24

1) Unlimited Submarine Warfare-Germany announced on Jaunary 31, 1917, that it would sink all ships, without warning in a large war zone off the coasts of the Allied nations in the eastern Atlantic and Mediterranean.
2) Zimmerman Telegram-The British intercepted a secret message from the German foreign secretary, Arthur Zimmerman, to the German minister in Mexico in which the Germans proposed that, in the event of war between the United States and Germany, Mexico attack the U.S. When the telegram was released to the press on March 1, 1917, many Americans became convinced that war with Germany was necessary.

Questions

Q25

When was the military draft enacted in World War I?

*Your Own Answer*_____

_____

Q26

Who commanded the American Expeditionary Force sent to to France in June 1917?

*Your Own Answer*_____

_____

Q27

When was the World War I armistice signed?

*Your Own Answer*_____

_____

Correct Answers

A25

The Selective Service Act was passed on May 18, 1917.

A26

Major General John J. Pershing

A27

November 11, 1918

Questions

Q28

What was the purpose of the War Industries Board?

*Your Own Answer*_____

Q29

a) What was the War Labor Board?
b) How did the war affect union membership?

*Your Own Answer*_____

Q30

How was the public mood affected by the war?

*Your Own Answer*_____

Correct Answers

A28

The War Industries Board coordinated industrial mobilization by allocating raw materials, standardizing manufactured products and instituting strict production and purchasing controls.

A29

a) The War Labor Board was created in April of 1918 to prevent strikes and work stoppages in war industries.
b) Union membership doubled during the war from about 2.5 million to 5 million.

A30

A number of volunteer organizations sprang up around the country to search for draft dodgers, enforce the sale of bonds, and report any opinion or conversation considered suspicious. Organizations such as the American Protective League who publicly humiliated people accused of not buying war bonds and persecuted, beat, and sometimes killed people of German descent.

Questions

Q31

Describe the Espionage and Sedition Acts.

Your Own Answer

Q32

What two Supreme Court cases upheld the constitutionality of the Espionage and Sedition Acts?

Your Own Answer

Q33

What was the major consequence of the war for blacks and other racial minorities?

Your Own Answer

Correct Answers

A31
The Espionage Act of 1917 provided for fines and imprisonment for persons who made false statements which aided the enemy, incited rebellion in the military, or obstructed recruitment or the draft. The Sedition Act of May 1918 forbade any criticism of the government, flag, or uniform, even if there were not detrimental consequences.

A32
The Espionage Act was upheld by the Supreme Court in the case of *Shenk v. United States* in 1919. The Sedition Act was similarly upheld in *Abrams v. United States* a few months later.

A33
About half a million rural southern blacks migrated to cities, mainly in the North and Midwest, to obtain employment in war and other industries, especially in steel and meat packing.

Questions

Q34

What was the name of President Wilson's peace plan and what was its primary message?

*Your Own Answer*_____

Q35

What was the consequence of the 1918 congressional elections on President Wilson's international stature?

*Your Own Answer*_____

Q36

What was President Wilson's biggest mistake concerning the Paris Peace Conference?

*Your Own Answer*_____

Correct Answers

A34
Wilson's plan was called the Fourteen Points and its primary message was that there should be peace without victory, meaning that the victors should not be vindictive toward the losers.

A35
Wilson had appealed to the voters to elect a Democratic Congress, saying to do otherwise would be a repudiation of his leadership in European affairs. The voters gave the Republicans a slim margin in both houses in the election, undermining his political support at home and his stature in the eyes of world leaders.

A36
Wilson did not appoint any Republican to the American delegation and did not consult Republican leadership in the Senate about the negotiations. Consequently, Wilson did not receive bipartisan support for his efforts at the conference.

Questions

Q37

Name four important provisions of the Versailles Treaty.

Your Own Answer_____

Q38

What was the main objection Republicans had to the League of Nations?

Your Own Answer_____

Q39

a) How did the Senate vote on the League of Nations?
b) How did Wilson's actions contribute to their vote?

Your Own Answer_____

Correct Answers

A37

1) The League of Nations was formed.
2) Germany was held responsible for causing the war. This decision was clearly contrary to the idea of peace without victory.
3) The new nations of eastern and central Europe partially fulfilled the idea of self-determination for all nationalities but the boundaries drawn at the conference left many people under the control of other nationalities.
4) German colonies were made mandates of the League of Nations and given in trusteeship to France, Japan, and Britain.

A38

The Republicans feared that Article X of the League Covenant would force the United States to go to war without the approval of Congress.

A39

a) On November 19, 1919, the treaty failed to get the two-thirds majority in the Senate.
b) After he suffered a severe stroke on October 2, Wilson took an uncompromisingly partisan approach to the treaty, ensuring its defeat. Many historians believe that Wilson's ill health impaired his judgement.

Questions

Q40

What did the Nineteenth Amendment provide for and when was it approved by Congress?

Your Own Answer

Q41

What factor contributed to the increased number of strikes in 1919?
a) In what city did the police strike?
b) Why did public support for striking workers diminish?

Your Own Answer

Q42

a) What was the primary reason for the Race Riots of 1919?
b) In what city was rioting the worst?

Your Own Answer

Correct Answers

A40

The Nineteenth Amendment provided for woman suffrage, and it was approved by Congress in 1919.

A41

The rapid postwar inflation contributed to the striking workers demand for higher wages.
a) Boston
b) The Communist Revolution of 1917 in Russia inspired in many Americans a fear of violence and revolution by workers.

A42

a) White hostility based on competition for lower paid jobs and black encroachment into neighborhoods.
b) The Chicago riot was the worst, lasting 13 days and leaving 38 dead, 520 wounded, and 1,000 families homeless.

Questions

Q43

a) Who were the Republican and Democratic nominees for president in 1920?
b) Who won?

Your Own Answer_____

Q44

In what industry was the moving assembly line first introduced?

Your Own Answer_____

Q45

a) What was the impact of the Federal Highway Act?
b) When was it passed?

Your Own Answer_____

Correct Answers

A43

a) The Republicans nominated Senator Warren G. Harding and the Democrats nominated Governor James Cox of Ohio.
b) Harding was elected President.

A44

It was introduced in the automobile industry by Henry Ford in 1913 and 1914.

A45

a) The Federal Highway Act started the federal highway system and gave matching funds to the states for construction.
b) 1916

Questions

Q46

The sale of what type of products was responsible for the prosperity of the 1920s?

Your Own Answer_____

Q47

What was the major business trend during the 1920s?

Your Own Answer_____

Q48

Why did farm expenses rise during the 1920s?

Your Own Answer_____

Correct Answers

A46

Consumer products, such as automobiles, refrigerators, and furniture

A47

The trend toward corporate consolidation

A48

Expenses rose with the cost of more sophisticated machinery and a greater use of chemical fertilizers.

Questions

Q49

What explains the tremendous growth of the suburbs during the 1920s?

Your Own Answer_____

Q50

How did technology and urbanization lead to a sharp rise in the standard of living during the 1920s?

Your Own Answer_____

Q51

What were some of the characteristics of the "Jazz Age" of the 1920s?

Your Own Answer_____

Correct Answers

A49
Better transportation through streetcars, commuter railroads, and automobiles as well as the easy availability of financing for home construction

A50
Technological conveniences such as electric stoves, vacuum cleaners, refrigerators, washing machines, and toasters made life less burdensome. Urban living improved access to electricity, natural gas, telephones, and piped water.

A51
Greater sexual promiscuity, drinking, and new forms of dancing considered erotic by the older generation

Questions

Q52

What ideas are associated with Marcus Garvey?

*Your Own Answer*_____

Q53

What was the average weekly movie attendance in 1929?

*Your Own Answer*_____

Q54

Explain the term "Lost Generation."

*Your Own Answer*_____

Correct Answers

A52

He advocated black racial pride, separatism, and a return of blacks to Africa rather than integration.

A53

90 million people

A54

The "Lost Generation" refers to the many talented writers of the twenties who were disgusted with the hypocrisy and materialism of contemporary American society. Examples of this group of writers include Ernest Hemingway, F. Scott Fitzgerald, Ezra Pound, and T.S. Eliot.

Questions

Q55

Describe the National Origin Act of 1924.

Your Own Answer

Q56

What explains the growth of organized crime during the 1920s?

Your Own Answer

Q57

What was the focus of the Scopes Trial?

Your Own Answer

Correct Answers

A55

This act was aimed to restrict immigration. The law set quotas at two percent of the number of foreign-born persons of that nationality in the United States in 1890, excluded all Orientals, and imposed an annual maximum of 164,000.

A56

Prohibition, because organized crime helped meet the demand for illegal alcohol

A57

The focus of the trial was whether evolution should be taught in the public schools. Although the defendant, a high school biology teacher named John Thomas Scopes, was convicted of violating a Tennessee law which forbid the teaching of evolution, the trial was largely seen as a victory for free speech.

Questions

Q58

Who were Sacco and Vanzetti?

Your Own Answer_____

Q59

When were the Revenue Acts passed and what did they do?

Your Own Answer_____

Q60

a) What products were affected by the Fordney McCumber Tariff?
b) What year was it passed?

Your Own Answer_____

Correct Answers

A58

Sacco and Vanzetti were Italian immigrants and admitted anarchists convicted of murder in 1920 and sentenced to death. Many believe their convictions were based on the political radicalism of the defendants, not evidence.

A59

The Revenue Acts were passed in 1921 and 1924, and they cut the maximum tax rates to 50 percent and then to 40 percent.

A60

a) The tariffs imposed high rates on farm products and protected such infant industries as rayon, china, toys, and chemicals.
b) 1922

Questions

Q61

Which law unified the federal budget for the first time?

Your Own Answer

Q62

Name the most famous scandal of the Harding administration.

Your Own Answer

Q63

In the election of 1924, who did the Republicans and Democrats nominate?
a) What new party was formed for this election?
b) Who was this new party's nominee?

Your Own Answer

Correct Answers

A61

The Budget and Accounting Act of 1921

A62

The most famous scandal of the Harding administration was the Teapot Dome Scandal. Secretary of the Interior Albert B. Fall was convicted, fined, and imprisoned for accepting bribes in exchange for leasing oil reserves at Teapot Dome.

A63

The Republicans nominated Calvin Coolidge, who had become president after Harding's death while the Democrats nominated John W. Davis, a conservative Wall Street lawyer.
a) The Progressive Party
b) Robert LaFollette

Questions

Q64

Name the order of finish in the 1924 presidential election.

*Your Own Answer*_____

Q65

What famous saying is associated with President Coolidge?

*Your Own Answer*_____

Q66

What were some of the features of the Revenue Act of 1926?

*Your Own Answer*_____

Correct Answers

A64

1) Coolidge
2) Davis
3) LaFollette

A65

"The business of the United States is business."

A66

It reduced the basic income tax, abolished the gift tax, and cut the estate tax in half.

Questions

Q67

What was controversial about 1928 Democratic presidential nominee, Alfred Smith?

Your Own Answer_____

Q68

Name the three treaties which resulted from the Washington Conference. Briefly describe each treaty.

Your Own Answer_____

Q69

What did the Dawes Plan do?

Your Own Answer_____

Correct Answers

A67

He was Catholic and against prohibition.

A68

1) Five Power Pact – ended new construction of capital naval vessels
2) Nine Power Pact – upheld the open door in China
3) Four Power Pact – bound the United States, Great Britain, Japan, and France to respect each other's possessions in the Pacific

A69

The Dawes Plan helped Germany, which was bankrupt, pay reparations to the Allies by having American banks make loans of $2.5 billion to Germany by 1930.

Questions

Q70

a) What was the Kellogg-Briand Pact?
b) What was its major flaw?

*Your Own Answer*_____

Q71

Cite several reasons for the stock market crash of 1929 and the Great Depression that followed.

*Your Own Answer*_____

Q72

Describe five economic effects of the Depression.

*Your Own Answer*_____

Correct Answers

A70

a) The Kellog-Briand Pact was a treaty signed at Paris in August 1928 which renounced war as an instrument of national policy.
b) The treaty had no enforcement provisions.

A71

Many people had bought stock on a margin of ten percent, meaning that they had borrowed 90 percent of the purchase through a broker's loan, and put up the stock as collateral.

A72

1) Unemployment rose to 25%.
2) National income dropped 54%.
3) Labor income fell about 41%.
4) Industrial production dropped about 51%.
5) 22% of the nation's banks failed by 1932.

Questions

Q73

What was the Hawley-Smoot Tariff?
a) When was it passed?
b) Why is it still considered controversial?

*Your Own Answer*_____

_____

Q74

What was the purpose of the Reconstruction Finance Cooperation (RFC)?

*Your Own Answer*_____

_____

Q75

a) What was the Garner-Wagner Bill?
b) Why did Hoover veto it?

*Your Own Answer*_____

_____

Correct Answers

A73

This law raised duties on both agricultural and manufacturers imports.
a) June 1930
b) Historians still argue over whether or not it contributed to the spread of the international depression

A74

Chartered by Congress in 1932, the RFC made loans to railroads, banks, and other financial institutions. Its aim was to prevent the failure of basic firms on which many other elements of the economy depended.

A75

a) The Garner-Wagner would have appropriated federal funds for relief of the needy.
b) Hoover vetoed the bill because he was philosophically opposed to using federal funds for that purpose.

Questions

Q76

What was the Bonus Army?
a) Why were they forced to leave Washington?
b) Who commanded the force which removed them?

*Your Own Answer*_____

Q77

Describe some of the features of the Democratic platform in the election of 1932

*Your Own Answer*_____

Q78

How many states did President Hoover carry in 1932?

*Your Own Answer*_____

Correct Answers

A76

The Bonus Army was a group of about 14,000 unemployed veterans who went to Washington in the summer of 1932 to lobby Congress for immediate payment of the bonus which had been approved in 1924 for payment in 1945.
a) After two veterans were killed in a clash with the police, Hoover, calling them insurrectionists and communists, ordered the army to remove them.
b) General Douglas MacArthur

A77

Some of the features were a repeal of prohibition, government aid for the unemployed, and a 25 percent cut in government spending.

A78

Six

Questions

Q79

What state was Franklin D. Roosevelt governor of when he was elected president?

Your Own Answer_____

Q80

What were President Roosevelt's inner circle of unofficial advisers called?

Your Own Answer_____

Q81

What was the Twenty-first Amendment to the Constitution? When did it take effect?

Your Own Answer_____

Correct Answers

A79

New York

A80

The Brain Trust

A81

The Twenty-first Amendment repealed prohibition and it took effect in December 1933.

Questions

Q82

What memorable slogan did President Roosevelt use in his inaugural speech on March 4, 1933?

Your Own Answer___

Q83

What was the term used to describe the legislation passed between 1933 and 1935?

Your Own Answer___

Q84

Name the five pieces of legislation passed in 1933 to deal with the nation's banking crisis.

Your Own Answer___

Correct Answers

A82

"The only thing we have to fear is fear itself."

A83

The First New Deal

A84

1) Emergency Banking Relief Act
2) The Banking Act of 1933
3) The Truth-in Securities Act
4) The Home Owners Loan Corporation
5) Nation went off the gold standard

Questions

Q85

What was the purpose of the Securities and Exchange Commission?

*Your Own Answer*_____

Q86

Why was the Federal Housing Administration created?

*Your Own Answer*_____

Q87

a) What was the Federal Emergency Relief Act?
b) How was it administered?

*Your Own Answer*_____

Correct Answers

A85

To supervise stock exchanges and to punish fraud in securities trading

A86

It was created to insure long-term, low interest mortgages for home construction and repair.

A87

a) This law, passed in the first 100 days of the Roosevelt administration, appropriated $500 million for aid to the poor to be distributed by state and local governments.
b) It was administered by the Federal Emergency Relief administration.

Questions

Q88

a) Who was eligible to join the Civilian Conservation Corps?
b) What kind of work did the Corps do?

*Your Own Answer*_____

Q89

a) How did the Public Works Administration work?
b) What was its objective?

*Your Own Answer*_____

Q90

What did the Federal Farm Loan Act do?

*Your Own Answer*_____

Correct Answers

A88

a) Young men ages 18 to 24 from families on relief
b) They worked on flood control, soil conservation, and forest projects under the direction of the War Department.

A89

a) Federal money was distributed to state and local governments for building projects such as schools, highways, and hospitals.
b) The object was to "prime the pump" of the economy by creating construction jobs.

A90

It consolidated all farm credit programs into the Farm Credit Administration to make low interest loans for farm mortgages and other agricultural purposes.

Questions

Q91

When was the Commodity Credit Corporation established? What was their purpose?

*Your Own Answer*_____

Q92

Describe the Frazier-Lemke Farm Bankruptcy Act of 1934.

*Your Own Answer*_____

Q93

What was the aim of the National Industrial Recovery Act of 1934?

*Your Own Answer*_____

Correct Answers

A91

The Commodity Credit Corporation was established in October of 1933 to make loans to corn and cotton farmers against their crops so they could hold them for higher prices.

A92

This act allowed farmers to defer foreclosure on their land while they obtained new financing, and helped them to recover property already lost through easy financing.

A93

The act sought to stabilize the economy by preventing extreme competition, labor-management conflicts and overproduction.

Questions

Q94

a) What is the Tennessee Valley Authority (TVA)?
b) What did the TVA represent?

*Your Own Answer*_____

Q95

What were three common conservative criticisms of the First New Deal?

*Your Own Answer*_____

Q96

When did the Second New Deal begin?

*Your Own Answer*_____

Correct Answers

A94

a) The TVA, a public corporation under a three member board, built 20 dams to stop flooding and soil erosion, improve navigation, and generate hydroelectric power.
b) The TVA represented the first major experiment in regional public planning.

A95

1) Deficit financing
2) Federal spending for relief
3) Government regulation of business

A96

1935

Questions

Q97

Describe how the Works Progress Administration (WPA) worked.

*Your Own Answer*_____

Q98

What did the Rural Electrification Administration (REA) do?

*Your Own Answer*_____

Q99

a) What was the Wagner Act?
b) When was it enacted?

*Your Own Answer*_____

Correct Answers

A97

The WPA employed people from the relief rolls for thirty hours of work a week at pay double the relief payment but less than private employment. Most of the projects undertaken were in construction.

A98

It provided loans and WPA labor to electric co-operatives to build lines into rural areas not served by private companies.

A99

a) It reaffirmed labor's right to unionize, prohibited unfair labor practices, and created the National Labor Relations Board (NLRB) to oversee and insure fairness in labor-management relations.
b) May 1935

Questions

Q100

Describe the main provisions of the Social Security Act.

*Your Own Answer*_____

Q101

Explain the Banking Act of 1935.

*Your Own Answer*_____

Q102

What was the result of the Reserve Act of 1935?

*Your Own Answer*_____

Correct Answers

A100

The act established a retirement plan for persons over age 65 funded by a tax or wages paid equally by employee and employer. The act also provided matching funds to the states for aid to the blind, handicapped, and dependent children.

A101

The Banking Act of 1935 created a stong central Board of Governors of the Federal Reserve System with broad powers over the operations of the regional banks.

A102

It increased income taxes on higher incomes, and also inheritance, large gift, and capital gains tax.

Questions

Q103

In the 1936 election, President Roosevelt carried every state except two. Name them.

Your Own Answer

Q104

Describe the composition of the New Deal coalition.

Your Own Answer

Q105

What prompted President Roosevelt's ill-fated "court packing" proposal?

Your Own Answer

Correct Answers

A103

Maine and Vermont

A104

1) Solid South
2) Ethnic groups in big cities
3) Midwestern farmers
4) Union workers
5) Blacks

A105

He was frustrated over the refusal of older, conservative judges to retire.

Questions

Q106

When was the Wagner-Steagall Act passed? What did it do?

*Your Own Answer*_____

Q107

What was another term used to describe the Fair Labor Standards Act?

*Your Own Answer*_____

Q108

Why was President Roosevelt reluctant to support anti-lynching legislation?

*Your Own Answer*_____

Correct Answers

A106

The law was passed in 1937 and it established the United States Housing Authority (USHA), which could borrow money to lend to local agencies.

A107

The minimum wage law

A108

He was fearful of alienating the Southern wing of the Democratic Party.

Questions

Q109

a) What prompted President Roosevelt to issue an executive order establishing the Fair Employment Practice Committee in June of 1941?
b) What was the purpose of the committee?

*Your Own Answer*_____

Q110

What did the Indian Reorganization Act of 1934 do?

*Your Own Answer*_____

Q111

What prompted the division in the labor movement between the AFL and the CIO?

*Your Own Answer*_____

Correct Answers

A109

a) A threat by black union leader A. Philip Randolph to lead a black march on Washington to demand equal access to defense jobs
b) The purpose of the committee was to ensure consideration for minorities in defense employment.

A110

It restored tribal ownership of lands, recognized tribal constitutions and government, and provided loans to tribes for economic development.

A111

The CIO wanted to unionize the mass production industries, such as automobiles and rubber, with industrial unions while the AFL continued to try to organize workers in those industries by crafts.

Questions

Q112

John L. Lewis was the leader of what union?

Your Own Answer

Q113

By 1941, how many workers belonged to a union?

Your Own Answer

Q114

Identify the 1940 movie classic which commented on the Depression.

Your Own Answer

Correct Answers

A112

United Mine Workers

A113

8.7 million, or 41% of the workforce

A114

The Grapes of Wrath

Questions

Q115

What was the effect of radio on American culture?

*Your Own Answer*_____

Q116

What was the Good Neighbor Policy?

*Your Own Answer*_____

Q117

In what year did the United States recognize the Soviet Union?

*Your Own Answer*_____

Correct Answers

A115

It tended to make Americans more uniform in their attitudes, taste, speech, and humor.

A116

The attempt by the Roosevelt administration to improve relations with Latin American nations.

A117

1933

Questions

Q118

What was the Johnson Act of 1934?

*Your Own Answer*_____

Q119

What prompted the Neutrality Acts of 1935?

*Your Own Answer*_____

Q120

What did the Neutrality Acts of 1937 do?

*Your Own Answer*_____

Correct Answers

A118

When European nations stopped payment on World War I debts to the United States, this law prohibited any nation in default from selling securities to any American citizen or corporation.

A119

Isolationist sentiment

A120

The laws gave the president authority to determine if a civil war was a threat to world peace and covered by the Neutrality Acts, prohibited all arms sales to belligerents and allowed the cash and carry sale of nonmilitary goods to belligerents.

Questions

Q121

What was the United States response to the Manchurian Crisis?

*Your Own Answer*_____

Q122

In what year did Italy invade Ethiopia?

*Your Own Answer*_____

Q123

What treaty did Germany defy when it occupied the Rhineland in 1936?

*Your Own Answer*_____

Correct Answers

A121

President Hoover refused to consider economic or military sanctions. The only American action was to refuse recognition of Manchukuo, which the Japanese created.

A122

1936

A123

The Versailles Treaty

Questions

Q124

In what years did the following events occur?
a) The formation of the Rome-Berlin Axis
b) Japanese invasion of China
c) Union of Germany and Austria
d) German occupation of all of Czechoslovakia

Your Own Answer

Q125

In what year was the War Resources Board created? What was its purpose?

Your Own Answer

Q126

What was the aim of the America First Committee?

Your Own Answer

Correct Answers

A124

    a) 1936
    b) 1937
    c) 1938
    d) 1939

A125

The War Resources Board was created in 1939 by President Roosevelt to develop a plan for industrial mobilization in the event of war.

A126

To keep America out of World War II

Questions

Q127

What did the Selective Service and Training Act do?

*Your Own Answer*_____

Q128

What was significant about the Democrats nominating President Roosevelt for re-election in 1940?

*Your Own Answer*_____

Q129

What was the American Neutrality Patrol?

*Your Own Answer*_____

Correct Answers

A127

Approved in September of 1940, the act created the nation's first peacetime draft.

A128

Since Roosevelt was being nominated for a third term, it broke with a tradition that had existed since the time of Washington that presidents would only serve two terms.

A129

Begun in April of 1941, the American navy would search out but not attack German submarines in the western half of the Atlantic, and warn British vessels of their location.

Questions

Q130

What was the Atlantic Charter?

*Your Own Answer*_____

Q131

How did the United States respond to the German invasion of the Soviet Union?

*Your Own Answer*_____

Q132

How did the United States respond to Japan gaining military control of southern Indochina from Vichy France?

*Your Own Answer*_____

Correct Answers

A130

It was a statement of principles issued by President Roosevelt and Winston Churchill, the British Prime Minister, which described a postwar world based on self-determination for all nations. It also endorsed the principles of freedom of speech and religion and freedom from want and fear.

A131

It extended Lend-Lease Assistance to the Soviet Union.

A132

The U.S. responded by freezing Japanese funds in the United States, closing the Panama Canal to Japan, activating the Phillipine Militia and by placing an embargo on the export of oil and other vital products to Japan.

Questions

Q133

Instead of Pearl Harbor, where did most American leaders think Japan was going to attack?

Your Own Answer_____

Q134

How many American servicemen were killed at Pearl Harbor?

Your Own Answer_____

Q135

How did President Roosevelt describe the Japanese attack on Pearl Harbor?

Your Own Answer_____

Correct Answers

A133

Dutch East Indies and Malaya

A134

2,323

A135

"A day that would live in infamy"

Questions

Q136

What was Lend-Lease?
a) When was Lend-Lease passed?
b) What did it provide for?
c) What was its significance?

Your Own Answer

Q137

When was the General Maximum Price Regulation Act passed? What did it do?

Your Own Answer

Q138

Explain the Smith-Connolly Act.

Your Own Answer

Correct Answers

A136
a) March 1941
b) Made available $7 million for war materials that President Roosevelt could sell, lend, lease, exchange or transfer to any country whose defense he deemed vital to the United States.
c) Indicated that the U.S. was moving toward stronger support for Britain.

A137

The act was passed in April 1942, and it froze prices and extended rationing.

A138

Passed in 1943, the Smith-Connolly Antistrike Act authorized government seizure of a plant or mine idled by a strike if the war effort was impeded.

Questions

Q139

a) What Supreme Court decision upheld President Roosevelt's 1942 order that Japanese-Americans be relocated to concentration camps?
b) What year was the decision?
c) When were the camps closed?

Your Own Answer_____

Q140

What was the importance of the 1944 Supreme Court decision *Smith v. Millwright*?

Your Own Answer_____

Q141

When did President Roosevelt die?

Your Own Answer_____

Correct Answers

A139

a) *Korematsu v. United States*
b) 1944
c) March 1946

A140

This decision struck down the Texas primary elections, which were restricted to whites, for violating the Fiftteenth Amendment.

A141

April 12, 1945

Questions

Q142

a) When did the Battle of Kassarine Pass happen?
b) What was the outcome of the battle?

Your Own Answer_____

Q143

a) When did the Allied armies invade the Italian mainland?
b) When did Rome fall?

Your Own Answer_____

Q144

When was D-Day? What did it signify?

Your Own Answer_____

Correct Answers

A142

a) February 1943
b) The Allied army met General Erwin Rommel's Africa Korps and although the battle is variously interpreted as a standoff or a defeat for the U.S., Rommel's forces were soon trapped by the British moving in from Egypt.

A143

a) September 1943
b) June 1944

A144

D-Day was on June 6, 1944, and it signified the beginning of the liberation of Europe by the Allied forces.

Questions

Q145

What happened at the Battle of the Bulge? When did it happen?

*Your Own Answer*_____

_____

Q146

a) What was the Battle of the Coral Sea?
b) What was its significance?

*Your Own Answer*_____

_____

Q147

a) What happened at the Battle of Midway?
b) Why was it important?

*Your Own Answer*_____

_____

Correct Answers

A145

The Germans counter-attacked, driving the Allies back about 50 miles into Belgum. It began December 16, 1944. By January, the Allies were once more advancing toward Germany.

A146

a) This battle occured on May 7-8, 1942. Planes from the American carriers Lexington and Yorktown forced Japanese troop transports to turn back from attacking Port Moresby.
b) The significance is that the battle stopped the Japanese advance on Australia.

A147

a) American air power destroyed four Japanese carriers and about 300 planes.
b) The battle proved to be the turning point in the Pacific War.

Questions

Q148

What happened in Japan after the Battle of the Philippine Sea?

Your Own Answer_____

Q149

a) What battle saw the first use of Japanese kamikaze attacks?
b) When was this battle?

Your Own Answer_____

Q150

What was the significance of the Battle of Okinawa?

Your Own Answer_____

Correct Answers

A148

General Tojo resigned as premier of Japan.

A149

a) The Battle of Leyte Gulf
b) October 1944

A150

The battle virtually destroyed Japan's remaining defenses.

Questions

Q151

What was the Manhattan Project?

Your Own Answer_____

Q152

a) Where was the first atomic bomb exploded?
b) When was it exploded?

Your Own Answer_____

Q153

a) When was the atomic bomb dropped on Hiroshima?
b) What is the estimate for the number of people killed in the attack?

Your Own Answer_____

Correct Answers

A151

The project was established in August of 1942 for the purpose of developing an atomic bomb.

A152

a) Alamogordo, New Mexico
b) July 16, 1945

A153

a) August 6, 1945
b) 78,000

Questions

Q154

When did Japan announce its surrender?

*Your Own Answer*_____

Q155

a) When was the Casablanca Conference?
b) What was its significance?

*Your Own Answer*_____

Q156

What happened at the Moscow Conference in October 1943?

*Your Own Answer*_____

Correct Answers

A154

August 14, 1945

A155

a) January 14-25, 1943
b) During this conference, President Roosevelt and Prime Minister Churchill declared a policy of unconditional surrender for "all enemies".

A156

The Soviets agreed to enter the war against Japan after Germany was defeated and to participate in a work organization after the war.

Questions

Q157

a) When was the Declaration of Cairo issued?
b) What did it call for?

Your Own Answer_____

Q158

a) When was the Teheran Conference?
b) What happened there?

Your Own Answer_____

Q159

What did the Soviets agree to at the 1945 Yalta Conference?

Your Own Answer_____

Correct Answers

A157
a) December 1, 1943
b) It called for Japan's unconditional surrender and stated that all Chinese territories occupied by Japan would be returned to China and that Korea would be free and independent.

A158
a) November 28 to December 1, 1943
b) Stalin reaffirmed the Soviet commitment to enter the war against Japan and discussed coordination of the Soviet offensive with the Allied invasion of France.

A159
They agreed to enter the Pacific War within three months after Germany surrendered and agreed to the "Declaration of Liberated Europe" which called for free elections.

Questions

Q160

a) When was the Potsdam Conference?
b) What happened at the conference?

Your Own Answer_____

Q161

What famous speech was given in Fulton, Missouri in 1946?

Your Own Answer_____

Q162

What was the name of the United States policy toward the Soviet Union in the postwar era?

Your Own Answer_____

Correct Answers

A160

a) July 17 to August 2, 1945
b) The United States, Great Britain and the Soviet Union agreed to the concept of war crimes trials and the demilitarization and denazification of Germany.

A161

Winston Churchill's "Iron Curtain" speech, in which he stated that an Iron Curtain had spread across Europe separating the Democratic West from the Communist East.

A162

Containment

Questions

Q163

a) What was the Truman Doctrine?
b) In what two countries was it first involved?

Your Own Answer_____

Q164

What was the objective of the Marshall Plan?

Your Own Answer_____

Q165

How did the communists take over in Czechoslovakia?

Your Own Answer_____

Correct Answers

A163

a) The doctrine stated that the United States must support free peoples who were existing communist domination.
b) The doctrine was first invoked when the United States gave military and economic aid to Greece and Turkey in 1947.

A164

The Marshall Plan provided economic aid to help rebuild Europe as a means of preventing communist expansion.

A165

A Soviet sponsored coup d'etat in February of 1948

Questions

Q166

a) When was the NATO Alliance formed?
b) What did all of its members pledge?

*Your Own Answer*_____

Q167

What happened at the Bretton Woods conference in July of 1944?

*Your Own Answer*_____

Q168

When was the United Nations established?

*Your Own Answer*_____

Correct Answers

A166

a) April 1949
b) That an attack against one would be considered an attack against all.

A167

Representatives from Europe and the U.S. signed agreements for an international bank and a world monetary fund to stabilize international currencies and rebuild the economies of war-torn nations.

A168

June 1945

Questions

Q169

Who headed the Allied Control Council which governed Japan after the war?

*Your Own Answer*_____

Q170

a) When did the Communists take over China?
b) Who was the leader of the Communist forces?

*Your Own Answer*_____

Q171

Why did President Truman remove General McArthur from his command during the Korean War?

*Your Own Answer*_____

Correct Answers

A169

General Douglas McArthur

A170

a) 1949
b) Mao Tse-tung

A171

Because McArthur criticized the president for fighting a limited war. McArthur called for a naval blockade of China and bombing north of the Yalu River.

Questions

Q172

a) When was the Korean armistice signed?
b) What was the war's outcome?

Your Own Answer_____

Q173

Who was President Eisenhower's secretary of state?

Your Own Answer_____

Q174

When did the U.S explode its first hydrogen bomb?

Your Own Answer_____

Correct Answers

A172

a) June 1953
b) Korea was divided along virtually the same boundary that had existed prior to the war.

A173

John Foster Dulles

A174

November 1952

Questions

Q175

Who became the new Soviet leader after Stalin died in 1953?

Your Own Answer_____

Q176

a) What happened to Vietnam as a result of the Geneva Accords?
b) What role did the U.S. play after the accord's were signed?

Your Own Answer_____

Q177

a) When was the Suez Canal crisis?
b) What was its significance?

Your Own Answer_____

Correct Answers

A175

Nikita Khrushchev

A176

a) Vietnam was split along the 17th parallel into North and South Vietnam.
b) The United States supplied aid to South Vietnam.

A177

a) 1956
b) The U.S. refused to support its allies France, Great Britain, and Israel when they attacked Egypt after Egyptian leader Nasser nationalized the Canal.

Questions

Q178

What was the Eisenhower Doctrine?

*Your Own Answer*_____

Q179

What did Eisenhower and Krushchev voluntarily agree to in October 1958?

*Your Own Answer*_____

Q180

When did Krushchev first tour the United States?

*Your Own Answer*_____

Correct Answers

A178

It was a pledge made by President Eisenhower in January of 1957 that the U.S. was prepared to use armed force in the Middle East against Communist aggression.

A179

To voluntarily suspend atmospheric tests of atomic weapons

A180

September of 1959

Questions

Q181

What was the U-2 incident?

*Your Own Answer*_____

Q182

Why did the U.S. support the overthrow of President Guzman at Guatemala in 1954?

*Your Own Answer*_____

Q183

Why did Vice President Nixon have to call off his goodwill tour Latin America in 1958?

*Your Own Answer*_____

Correct Answers

A181

On May 1, 1960, an American U-2 spy plane was shot down over the Soviet Union. Eisenhower took responsibility for the spy plane and Kruschev angrily called off the Paris summit conference which was to take place in a few days.

A182

He began accepting arms from the Soviet Union.

A183

Because of hostile mobs in Venezuela and Peru

Questions

Q184

How did the United States respond to Cuba signing a trade agreement with the Soviet Union in February of 1960?

*Your Own Answer*_____

_____

Q185

a) What was the Employment Act of 1946?
b) What was its primary goal?

*Your Own Answer*_____

_____

Q186

a) When was the Atomic Energy Commission created?
b) What did it do?

*Your Own Answer*_____

_____

Correct Answers

A184

The U.S. prohibited the importation of Cuban sugar in October of 1960 and breaking off diplomatic relations in January of 1961.

A185

a) This act established a three member council of economic advisors to evaluate the economy and advise the president and set up a congressional joint committee on the economic report.
b) Maintaining maximum employment

A186

a) 1946
b) It established civilian control over nuclear development and gave the president sole authority over the use of atomic weapons in warfare.

Questions

Q187

How did President Truman avert a railway strike in 1946?

*Your Own Answer*_____

Q188

What did the GI. Bill of 1944 do?

*Your Own Answer*_____

Q189

How did the 1947 Taft-Hartley Act affect unions?

*Your Own Answer*_____

Correct Answers

A187

He averted the strike by having the government take over the railroads and threatening to draft strikers into the army.

A188

It provided returning servicemen with $13 billion in aid ranging from education to housing.

A189

It made the "closed shop" illegal; ended the practice of employers collecting dues for unions; and forbade such actions as secondary boycotts, jurisdictional strikes, and feather bedding.

Questions

Q190

Explain the National Security Act of 1947.

*Your Own Answer*_____

Q191

a) When was the Twenty-second Amendment to the Constitution ratified?
b) What did it do?

*Your Own Answer*_____

Q192

How was the Democratic party split in 1948?

*Your Own Answer*_____

Correct Answers

A190

This act created a National Military Establishment, National Security Council, Joint Chiefs of Staff, and Central Intelligence Agency. Together these organizations were intended to coordinate the armed forces and intelligence services.

A191

a) 1951
b) Limited the president to two terms

A192

Many southern Democrats, angered by Truman's support of civil rights, split off to form the Dixiecrat Party headed by South Carolina Governor Strom Thurmond. The Progressive Party nominated former Vice President Henry Wallace for president and was formed as a protest against the cold war policies of the Truman administration.

Questions

Q193

What was the Fair Deal Program?

*Your Own Answer*_____

Q194

a) What was the Smith Act of 1940?
b) How was it used by the Truman administration during the Cold War?

*Your Own Answer*_____

Q195

a) What was the purpose of the Loyalty Review Board?
b) Why was it created?

*Your Own Answer*_____

Correct Answers

A193

It was Truman's proposals to enlarge and extend the New Deal. Some of its provisions included increasing the minimum wage, extending social security, and building more public housing.

A194

a) It made it illegal to advocate the overthrow of the government by force or to belong to an organization advocating such a position.
b) To jail leaders of the American Communist Party

A195

a) To review the patriotism and loyalty of government employees
b) It was created in response to criticism that the Truman administration was soft on Communism.

Questions

Q196

a) What was the McCarren Internal Security Act?
b) How was it viewed by President Truman?

*Your Own Answer*_____

Q197

What happened in the Rosenberg Case?

*Your Own Answer*_____

Q198

a) What were the results of the 1952 presidential election?
b) What was especially significant about the election?

*Your Own Answer*_____

Correct Answers

A196

a) This act required Communist front organizations to register with the attorney general and prevented their members from doing defense work.
b) It was passed over Truman's veto.

A197

In 1950, Julius and Ethel Rosenberg were charged with giving atomic secrets to the Soviet Union. They were convicted and executed in 1953.

A198

a) Republican Dwight Eisenhower defeated Democrat Adlai Stevenson.
b) For the first time since Reconstruction, the Republicans won some southern states.

Questions

Q199

What did the Atomic Energy Act of 1954 do?

Your Own Answer_____

Q200

Who did President Eisenhower appoint to be Chief Justice of the Supreme Court in 1953?

Your Own Answer_____

Q201

a) When did the Soviet Union launch *Sputnik*?
b) What were some of the consequences in the United States?

Your Own Answer_____

Correct Answers

A199

It allowed the construction of private nuclear power plants under Atomic Energy Commission license and oversight.

A200

Earl Warren

A201

a) October 4, 1957
b) It created fear that the U.S. was falling behind technologically and, as a result, in 1958 Congress established NASA to coordinate research and development and the National Defense Education Act to provide grants and loans for education.

Questions

Q202

What was the purpose of the Landrum-Griffen Labor-Management Act?

Your Own Answer

Q203

In what year did Alaska and Hawaii become states?

Your Own Answer

Q204

What was the meaning of the Supreme Court case *Brown v. Board of Education*?

Your Own Answer

Correct Answers

A202

It sought to control unfair union practices by establishing such rules as penalties for misuse of funds.

A203

1959

A204

In 1954, the court declared that separate educations facilities were inherently unequal and that states had to integrate with "all deliberate speed."

Questions

Q205

What did the Civil Rights Act of 1957 establish?

*Your Own Answer*_____

Q206

What was generally considered the pivotal events of the 1960 presidential election?

*Your Own Answer*_____

Q207

How much did economic productivity increase between 1945 and 1955?

*Your Own Answer*_____

Correct Answers

A205

It established a permanent Civil Rights Commission and a Civil Rights Division of the Justice Department which was empowered to prevent interference with the right to vote.

A206

A series of televised debates between John F. Kennedy and Richard Nixon which helped create a positive image for Kennedy

A207

35 percent

Questions

Q208

What was the fastest growing consumer product in the 1950s?

Your Own Answer_____

Q209

What technological factor explains the population growth of the Sun Belt in the post-war era?

Your Own Answer_____

Q210

Who pioneered the mass-produced housing development in the 1950s?

Your Own Answer_____

Correct Answers

A208

Television

A209

Increased use of air conditioning

A210

William Levitt

Questions

Q211

Explain the demographic trend called "white flight."

*Your Own Answer*_____

Q212

What was a popular critique of corporate culture in the 1950s?

*Your Own Answer*_____

Q213

What was the role of women in society immediately after World War II?

*Your Own Answer*_____

Correct Answers

A211

As blacks moved into the Northern and Midwestern cities, whites moved to the suburbs.

A212

That such environments encouraged the managerial personality and corporate cooperation rather than individualism.

A213

A cult of female domesticity re-emerged. Countless magazine articles promoted the concept that a woman's place was in the home.

Questions

Q214

How many Americans belonged to a church by 1960?

*Your Own Answer*_____

Q215

What was the social message in John Keats' *The Crack in the Picture Window* (1956)?

*Your Own Answer*_____

Q216

a) What was the theme of Arthur Miller's *Death of a Salesman*?
b) When was it written?

*Your Own Answer*_____

Correct Answers

A214

65 percent

A215

The book criticized the homogeneity of suburban life in the new mass-produced communities.

A216

a) The loneliness of the externally-directed person
b) 1949

Questions

Q217

Who were the Beats?

*Your Own Answer*_____

Q218

Why was President Kennedy unable to get much of his program through Congress?

*Your Own Answer*_____

Q219

What was the Area Redevelopment Act of 1961?

*Your Own Answer*_____

Correct Answers

A217

They were a group of young writers in the 1950s alienated by twentieth-century life who emphasized alcohol, drugs, sex, jazz, and Buddhism.

A218

Because of the alliance between Republicans and Southern Democrats

A219

It made available nearly $400 million in loans to "distressed areas".

Questions

Q220

What did the 1961 Housing Act provide?

*Your Own Answer*_____

Q221

Who were the "Freedom Riders?"

*Your Own Answer*_____

Q222

What was the 1963 March on Washington?

*Your Own Answer*_____

Correct Answers

A220

It provided nearly $5 billion over four years for the preservation of open spaces, development of mass transit, and the construction of middle-class housing.

A221

They were a group of blacks and whites who traveled across the south in 1961 to test federal enforcement of regulation prohibiting discrimination.

A222

It was a demonstration by over 200,000 people in support of the 1963 Civil Rights Bill. It was at this demonstration that Martin Luther King gave his famous "I Have a Dream" speech.

Questions

Q223

What was the Bay of Pigs operation?

*Your Own Answer*_____

Q224

What was the Nuclear Test Ban Treaty?

*Your Own Answer*_____

Q225

a) What did the Alliance for Progress provide?
b) When did it start?

*Your Own Answer*_____

Correct Answers

A223

Under Eisenhower, the C.I.A. trained some 2,000 men for an invasion of Cuba to overthrow Fidel Castro on April 19, 1961 this force invaded at the Bay of Pigs but was pinned down and forced to surrender.

A224

In July 1963, a treaty banning the atmospheric testing of nuclear weapons was signed by all the major powers except France and China.

A225

a) It provided $20 million in aid for Latin America.
b) 1961

Questions

Q226

a) How did President Kennedy respond to the building of Soviet missile sites in Cuba?
b) What year did this happen?
c) How was it resolved?

*Your Own Answer*_____

Q227

a) When was the Peace Corps established?
b) What was its purpose?

*Your Own Answer*_____

Q228

When was President Kennedy assassinated?

*Your Own Answer*_____

Correct Answers

A226

a) He announced a blockade of Cuba and called on Khruschev to dismantle the missile base.
b) 1962
c) Khruschev backed down and withdrew the missiles.

A227

a) 1961
b) It sent young volunteers to third world countries to contribute their skills in locally sponsored projects

A228

November 22, 1963

Questions

Q229

Name the most important provisions of the 1964 Civil Rights Act.

Your Own Answer

Q230

What was the aim of the Economic Opportunity Act of 1964?

Your Own Answer

Q231

What was the Medicare Act of 1965?

Your Own Answer

Correct Answers

A229
It outlawed racial discrimination by employers and unions, created the Equal Employment Opportunity Commission to enforce the law, and eliminated the remaining restrictions on black voting.

A230
It sought to eliminate poverty by establishing a Job Corps, community action programs, educational programs, work-study programs, job training, loans for small businesses, and VISTA, "a domestic peace corps".

A231
It combined hospital insurance for retired people with a voluntary plan to cover physician bills.

Questions

Q232

What important education bill was passed in 1965?

*Your Own Answer*_____

Q233

What was the effect of the Immigration Act of 1965?

*Your Own Answer*_____

Q234

How was rural poverty addressed in 1966?

*Your Own Answer*_____

Correct Answers

A232

The Elementary and Secondary Education Act, which provided $1.5 billion to school districts to improve the education of poor people

A233

It discontinued the national origin system and resulted in much higher levels of immigration from non-European countries.

A234

The Appalachian Regional Development Act of 1966 provided $1.1 billion for isolated mountain areas.

Questions

Q235

What was the conclusion of the Kerner Commission about the cause of the racial riots of the 1960s?

Your Own Answer

Q236

Who assassinated Martin Luther King?

Your Own Answer

Q237

Who unionized Mexican-American farm workers?

Your Own Answer

Correct Answers

A235

It concluded that the riots were directed at a social system that prevented blacks from getting good jobs and crowded them into ghettos.

A236

James Earl Ray

A237

Cesar Chavez

Questions

Q238

Describe the origins of the Free Speech Movement on American college campuses.

Your Own Answer

Q239

What was the leading New Left Student group during the 1960s?

Your Own Answer

Q240

What was the difference between the counterculture and the New Left?

Your Own Answer

Correct Answers

A238

Students at the University of California, Berkeley staged sit-ins in 1964 to protest the prohibition of political canvassing on campus. Led by Mario Savio, the movement changed from emphasizing student rights to criticizing the bureaucracy of American society.

A239

Students for a Democratic Society (SDS)

A240

Like the New Left, the founders of the counter culture were alienated by bureaucracy, materialism, and the Vietnam War, but they turned away from politics in favor of an alternative society.

Questions

Q241

a) Who wrote *The Feminine Mystique* in 1963?
b) What was the main point of the book?

Your Own Answer

Q242

When was the National Organization for Women founded?

Your Own Answer

Q243

a) What prompted the Gulf of Tonkin resolution in 1964?
b) What did the resolution do?

Your Own Answer

Correct Answers

A241
a) Betty Friedan
b) That middle-class society stifled women and did not allow them to use their individual talents.

A242
1966

A243
a) An alleged attack by North Vietnamese gunboats on American destroyers
b) It authorized President Johnson to use military force in Vietnam.

Questions

Q244

What was operation Rolling Thunder?

*Your Own Answer*_____

Q245

What was the "Domino Theory?"

*Your Own Answer*_____

Q246

a) What happened during the Tet offensive?
b) When was it?
c) What was its significance?

*Your Own Answer*_____

Correct Answers

A244

The first sustained American bombing of North Vietnam

A245

It was the theory which justified American involvement in Vietnam by arguing that if Vietnam fell, all of Southeast Asia would eventually go.

A246

a) The Vietcong attacked numerous South Vietnamese cities and towns, American bases, and even Saigon.
b) January 1968
c) Although they suffered large losses, the Vietcong won a psychological victory as American opinion began turning against the war.

Questions

Q247

a) What was the major issue in Eugene McCarthy's 1968 presidential campaign?
b) What was the significance of McCarthy's performance in the New Hampshire primary?

Your Own Answer

Q248

Who assassinated Robert Kennedy?

Your Own Answer

Q249

What explains the appeal of Governor George Wallace in the 1968 presidential election?

Your Own Answer

Correct Answers

A247

a) Opposition to the Vietnam War
b) McCarthy's surprisingly strong second place showing contributed to President Johnson's withdrawal from the race.

A248

Sirhan Sirhan

A249

Fears generated by protestors, black militants, and an expanding bureaucracy

Questions

Q250

What was the order of finish in the 1968 presidential election?

Your Own Answer_____

Q251

Who did President Nixon appoint to be Chief Justice of the Supreme Court?

Your Own Answer_____

Q252

What was President Nixon's New Federalism?

Your Own Answer_____

Correct Answers

A250

1) Richard Nixon
2) Hubert Humphrey
3) George Wallace

A251

Warren Burger

A252

It was a revenue sharing plan passed in 1972 to distribute $30 billion of federal revenue to the states.

Questions

Q253

When was the voting age lowered to 18?

*Your Own Answer*_____

Q254

What factors contributed to the economic slump of the early 1970s?

*Your Own Answer*_____

Q255

What were the two important economic initiatives made by President Nixon in 1971?

*Your Own Answer*_____

Correct Answers

A253

1970

A254

a) Federal deficits
b) International competition
c) Rising energy costs

A255

He announced a 90-day price and wage freeze, and he took the U.S. off the gold standard.

Questions

Q256

What was "Vietnamization?"

Your Own Answer_____

Q257

When was the military draft abolished?

Your Own Answer_____

Q258

What happened at Kent State in May 1970?

Your Own Answer_____

Correct Answers

A256

President Nixon's policy of building up South Vietnamese forces while gradually withdrawing American troops

A257

1973

A258

Four anti-war student protesters were killed by the National Guard.

Questions

Q259

What were the Pentagon Papers?

*Your Own Answer*_____

Q260

What were the three key elements of the peace treaty negotiated in 1972 between the U.S. and North Vietnam?

*Your Own Answer*_____

Q261

When did the last American combat troops leave South Vietnam?

*Your Own Answer*_____

Correct Answers

A259

Classified Defense Department documents published in 1971, against the protests of the Nixon administration, which revealed that the government had misled the Congress and the American people regarding its intentions in Vietnam durng the mid-1960s.

A260

1) A cease-fire
2) Return of American prisoners of war
3) Withdrawal of U.S. forces from Vietnam

A261

March 1973

Questions

Q262

What bold diplomatic initiatives did President Nixon begin in 1972?

*Your Own Answer*_____

Q263

What was the SALT Treaty of 1972?

*Your Own Answer*_____

Q264

What was "detente?"

*Your Own Answer*_____

Correct Answers

A262

He sent National Security Advisor Henry Kissinger on secret missions to plan summit meetings in both China and the Soviet Union.

A263

The Strategic Arms Limitation Treaty (SALT) was signed by the United States and the Soviet Union in 1972 in which both sides agreed to stop making ballistic missiles and to reduce the number of antiballistic missiles to 200 for each power.

A264

A policy initiated during the Nixon administration which aimed to reduce the amount of tension between the United States and the Soviet Union

Questions

Q265

a) What was OPEC?
b) How did it affect the United States?

Your Own Answer_____

Q266

What was the one state carried by George McGovern in the 1972 presidential election?

Your Own Answer_____

Q267

a) When was the Watergate break-in?
b) What happened at the break-in?

Your Own Answer_____

Correct Answers

A265

a) OPEC was a cartel of oil producing countries – Venezuela, Saudi Arabia, Kuwait, Iraq, and Iran – which significantly raised oil prices in the early 1970s.
b) OPEC's actions doubled gas prices in the U.S. and raised inflation above 10 percent.

A266

Massachusetts

A267

a) June 17, 1972
b) Four men associated with President Nixon's re-election campaign broke into Democratic headquarters and the Watergate apartment complex and were caught going through files and installing eavesdropping devices.

Questions

Q268

Why did Vice President Agnew resign in October of 1973?

Your Own Answer

Q269

a) When did President Nixon resign?
b) Who succeeded him?

Your Own Answer

Q270

What did the War Powers Act of 1973 accomplish?

Your Own Answer

Correct Answers

A268

He was accused of income tax fraud and having accepted bribes while a local official in Maryland.

A269

a) August 8, 1974
b) Vice President Gerald Ford

A270

It required congressional approval of any commitment of combat troops beyond 90 days.

Questions

Q271

What did the Freedom of Information Act do?

Your Own Answer

Q272

When was President Nixon pardoned?

Your Own Answer

Q273

What was the size of the federal budget deficit in 1976?

Your Own Answer

Correct Answers

A271

It required the government to act promptly when asked for information and to prove its case for classification when attempting to withhold information on grounds of national security.

A272

September 1974

A273

$60 billion

Questions

Q274

When did Saigon fall to the North Vietnamese?

*Your Own Answer*_____

Q275

What was the Mayaguez Crisis of 1975?

*Your Own Answer*_____

Q276

Who opposed President Ford for the Republican nomination in 1976?

*Your Own Answer*_____

Correct Answers

A274

April 1975

A275

Cambodia seized the American merchant ship *Mayaguez* in the Gulf of Siam. In response, President Ford ordered a marine assault, which liberated the ship and crew but 38 marines were killed as a result.

A276

Former California Governor Ronald Reagan

Questions

Q277

What was a common criticism of the Carter administration?

Your Own Answer_____

Q278

a) When was the Panama Canal Treaty negotiated?
b) What did it provide?

Your Own Answer_____

Q279

When did the United States recognize the People's Republic of China?

Your Own Answer_____

Correct Answers

A277

Carter proposed complex programs to Congress and then did not support them through the legislative power

A278

a) 1978
b) It provided for the transfer of ownership of the Canal to Panama in 1999 and guaranteed its neutrality.

A279

1979

Questions

Q280

What was the fate of the SALT II Treaty?

Your Own Answer_____

Q281

What were the major provisions of the 1978 Camp David Accords?

Your Own Answer_____

Q282

How did the United States respond to the Soviet invasion of Afghanistan?

Your Own Answer_____

Correct Answers

A280

It never passed the Senate.

A281

Israel promised to return occupied land in the Sinai to Egypt in exchange for Egyptian recognition.

A282

The Carter administration stopped shipments of grain to the Soviet Union, withdrew SALT II from the Senate, and withdrew the U.S. from the 1980 Moscow Olympics.

Questions

Q283

Why did Iranian "students" take over the U.S. Embassy in November 1979?

Your Own Answer

Q284

What was the consequence of the failed U.S. rescue attempt of the hostages in Iran in April of 1980?

Your Own Answer

Q285

Who challenged President Carter for the Democratic nomination in 1980?

Your Own Answer

Correct Answers

A283

Because the U.S. had allowed the exiled Shah of Iran to come to the U.S. for medical treatment, the Iranians demanded that the Shah be returned to Iran for trial.

A284

Secretary of State Cyrus Vance resigned in protest.

A285

Senator Edward M. Kennedy

Questions

Q286

There was a three way race for the presidency in 1980. Name the order of finish.

Your Own Answer

Q287

What two important events happened on January 20, 1981?

Your Own Answer

Q288

What happened to the proposed Equal Rights Amendment?

Your Own Answer

Correct Answers

A286

1) Ronald Reagan
2) Jimmy Carter
3) John Anderson

A287

President Reagan was inaugurated, and the hostages were released from Iran.

A288

It was approved by Congress in 1972 but never ratified by the required 38 states.

Questions

Q289

What did the Supreme Court decide in its 1973 *Roe v. Wade* decision?

Your Own Answer

Q290

What phrase was used to describe the 1970s generation?

Your Own Answer

Q291

What were the positions of the "Moral Majority" political movement?

Your Own Answer

Correct Answers

A289

It legalized abortion during the first three months of pregnancy.

A290

The "Me Generation"

A291

They favored prayer in school, opposed abortion and the ERA, and supported a strong national defense.

Questions

Q292

What three popular movies released in the late 1970s focus on the Vietnam War?

*Your Own Answer*_____

Q293

What was the theory behind supply-side economics?

*Your Own Answer*_____

Q294

What were the main provisions of the 1981 Economic Recovery Act?

*Your Own Answer*_____

Correct Answers

A292

1) *The Deer Hunter*
2) *Coming Home*
3) *Apocalypse Now*

A293

If government left more money in the hands of the people, they would invest rather than spend the excess consumer goods. The results would be greater production, more jobs, and greater prosperity.

A294

A 25 percent income tax cut spread over three years, reductions in capital gains, gift, and inheritance taxes, and business taxes were liberalized.

Questions

Q295

What was the major thrust in the Budget Reconciliation Act of 1981?

Your Own Answer

Q296

What was the size of the federal budget deficit by 1983?

Your Own Answer

Q297

What did the Deficit Reduction Act of 1984 do?

Your Own Answer

Correct Answers

A295

Congress cut $39 billion from domestic programs while increasing the defense budget by $12 billion.

A296

$195 billion

A297

It increased taxes by $50 billion.

Questions

Q298

Who attempted to assassinate President Reagan?

Your Own Answer

Q299

Who was the first woman appointed to the Supreme Court?

Your Own Answer

Q300

What was a major problem with President Reagan's appointed officials?

Your Own Answer

Correct Answers

A298

John Hinckley Jr.

A299

Sandra Day O'Connor

A300

More than 100 of his officials had been involved in scandals.

Questions

Q301

What happened in Grenada in 1983?

*Your Own Answer*_____

Q302

What was the consequence of American peace-keeping troops being sent into Lebanon?

*Your Own Answer*_____

Q303

What was the Democratic presidential ticket in 1984?

*Your Own Answer*_____

Correct Answers

A301

President Reagan sent troops onto the island to overthrow a newly established Cuban-backed regime.

A302

In October of 1983, a Moslem drove a truck filled with explosives into a building housing marines, killing 239. A few months later, Reagan removed all American troops from Lebanon.

A303

Walter Mondale and Geraldine Ferraro

Questions

Q304

What was the only state that Mondale carried in 1984?

*Your Own Answer*_____

Q305

a) Who became the new Soviet premier in March of 1985?
b) What were the characteristics of the new regime?

*Your Own Answer*_____

Q306

a) What was SDI?
b) What was its fate?

*Your Own Answer*_____

Correct Answers

A304

Minnesota

A305

a) Mikhail Gorbachev
b) A more flexible approach toward both domestic and foreign affairs

A306

a) A computer controlled strategic defense initiative, popularly called Star Wars, that would destroy enemy missiles from outerspace
b) Congress balked, skeptical about the technological possibilities and fearing enormous costs.

Questions

Q307

When were medium range missiles eliminated from Europe?

*Your Own Answer*_____

Q308

What were the major provisions of the Tax Reform Act of 1986?

*Your Own Answer*_____

Q309

What was the inflation rate in 1986?

*Your Own Answer*_____

Correct Answers

A307

December 1987

A308

It lowered tax rates, changing the highest rate on personal income from 50 percent to 28 percent and corporate taxes from 46 percent to 34 percent. At the same time, it removed many tax shelters and tax credits.

A309

22 percent

Questions

Q310

How did falling oil prices affect American banks in the late 1980s?

*Your Own Answer*_____

Q311

What were the main features of the Reagan administration farm policy?

*Your Own Answer*_____

Q312

What explains the rising U.S. trade deficits of the 1980s?

*Your Own Answer*_____

Correct Answers

A310

American banks suffered when oil-related international loans went unpaid.

A311

It reduced price supports and opposed debt relief passed by Congress.

A312

U.S. management and engineering skills had fallen behind Japan and Germany and the U.S. provided an open market to foreign businesses.

Questions

Q313

What explains the corporate merger phenomenon of the 1980s?

*Your Own Answer*_____

Q314

What happened on October 19, 1987, or "Black Monday?"

*Your Own Answer*_____

Q315

What event in 1986 damaged NASA's credibility?

*Your Own Answer*_____

Correct Answers

A313

1) Deregulation policies of the Reagan administration
2) The emerging international economy
3) It was fueled by funds released by new tax breaks.

A314

The Dow Jones stock market average dropped over 500 points.

A315

The explosion of the space shuttle *Challenger*

Questions

Q316

Who did President Reagan appoint to chief justice of the Supreme Court in 1986?

Your Own Answer

Q317

Who did the Republicans and Democrats nominate for president in 1988?

Your Own Answer

Q318

What was Bush's famous "pledge" during the 1988 campaign?

Your Own Answer

Correct Answers

A316

Associate Justice William Rehnquist

A317

The Republicans nominated George Bush while the Democrats nominated Michael Dukakis.

A318

"No new taxes"

Questions

Q319

How many states did Bush win in 1988?

Your Own Answer_____

Q320

How did the Bush administration respond to the reduced threat from the Soviet Union?

Your Own Answer_____

Q321

In 1989, President Bush signed into law an increase in the minimum wage. What was the new rate?

Your Own Answer_____

Correct Answers

A319

40

A320

In 1990, the Bush administration proposed to cut military spending by 10 percent and the armed forces by 25 percent.

A321

$4.25 per hour to be effective in 1991

Questions

Q322

What was the cause of the financial problems of the Savings and Loan industry in the late 1980s?

*Your Own Answer*_____

_____

Q323

How did Drexel Burnham Lambert violate the law during the Financial Market scandals of the 1980s?

*Your Own Answer*_____

_____

Q324

How did the Federal Reserve attempt to stimulate the economy in 1991?

*Your Own Answer*_____

_____

Correct Answers

A322

Bad real estate loans

A323

He pleaded guilty to insider trading, stock manipulation, and falsification of records.

A324

The Federal Reserve lowered interest rates.

Questions

Q325

a) What happened to the *Exxon Valdez* in 1989?
b) How was the incident resolved?

Your Own Answer

Q326

Why did Speaker of the House Jim Wright resign in 1989?

Your Own Answer

Q327

How did flag burning become a political issue in 1989?

Your Own Answer

Correct Answers

A325

a) The *Exxon Valdez* spilled more than 240,000 barrels of oil into Alaska's Prince William Sound in March of 1989.
b) Exxon was required to pay $1.025 billion in fines and restitution through the year 2001.

A326

He had violated rules regulating acceptance of gifts and outside income.

A327

In May 1989, the Supreme Court ruled that the Constitution protected protesters who burned the United States flag.

Questions

Q328

a) What was the Medicare Catastrophic Coverage Act of 1988?
b) Why was it controversial?

*Your Own Answer*_____

Q329

a) What was the objective of the 1990 Clear Air Act?
b) What were some of its provisions?

*Your Own Answer*_____

Q330

What was the 1990 Americans with Disabilities Act?

*Your Own Answer*_____

Correct Answers

A328
a) It placed a cap on fees Medicare patients paid to physicians and hospitals
b) Many senior citizens objected to the surtax that funded the program and, as a result, Congress appealed the act in 1989.

A329
a) To reduce the level of emissions by 50 percent by the year 2000
b) Cleaner gasolines were to be developed; cities were to reduce ozone; and nitrogen oxide emissions were to be cut one-third.

A330
A law barring discrimination against people with physical or mental disabilities

Questions

Q331

What did the 1991 Civil Rights Act establish?

*Your Own Answer*_____

Q332

Name the two justices appointed by President Bush to the Supreme Court.

*Your Own Answer*_____

Q333

What did the Cable Television Consumer Protection and Competition Act of 1992 establish?

*Your Own Answer*_____

Correct Answers

A331

It required employers in discrimination suits to prove that their hiring practices were not discriminatory.

A332

David Souter and Clarence Thomas

A333

It gave the federal government power to regulate cable television rates.

Questions

Q334

What was the justification for the United States invasion of Panama in 1989?

Your Own Answer_____

_____

Q335

Why did the United States lift its economic sanctions against Nicaragua in 1990?

Your Own Answer_____

_____

Q336

Why did China declare martial law in June of 1989?

Your Own Answer_____

_____

Correct Answers

A334

The alleged involvement of Panamanian dictator Manuel Noriega in the drug traffic between South America and the United States

A335

Because the leftist Sandinistas were removed from power through a presidential election.

A336

To crack down on pro-democracy demonstrators in Beijing

Questions

Q337

Why did the United States send marines into Liberia in August of 1990?

Your Own Answer_____

_____

Q338

What was the first Eastern European country to shift away from Communism in 1989?

Your Own Answer_____

_____

Q339

What event symbolized the collapse of Communism in Eastern Europe?

Your Own Answer_____

_____

Correct Answers

A337

To rescue Americans threatened by civil war

A338

Poland

A339

The fall of the Berlin Wall in 1989

Questions

Q340

a) Who became president of Czechoslovakia in 1989 after the Communists relinquished power?
b) What was his background?

Your Own Answer___

Q341

What did the START Treaty of 1990 accomplish?

Your Own Answer___

Q342

How did Iraq justify its 1990 invasion of Kuwait?

Your Own Answer___

Correct Answers

A340

a) Vaclav Havel
b) A playwright

A341

It cut U.S. and Soviet nuclear arsenals by 30 percent.

A342

That Kuwait had conspired with the United States to keep oil prices low.

Questions

Q343

How did the United States respond to the Iraqi invasion of Kuwait?

Your Own Answer_____

_____

Q344

How did the United States increase its commitment in the Persian Gulf in November of 1990?

Your Own Answer_____

_____

Q345

a) When did the Gulf War begin?
b) What was the name of the operation?

Your Own Answer_____

_____

Correct Answers

A343

By sending 100,000 troops to Saudi Arabia as part of Operation Desert Shield

A344

It increased the number of American troops in the region to more than 400,000 and set a January 15, 1991 deadline for Iraqi withdrawal from Kuwait.

A345

a) January 17, 1991
b) Operation Desert Storm

Questions

Q346

a) How did Iraq respond to the initial Allied air assault?
b) What was the purpose of this action?

*Your Own Answer*_____

_____

Q347

a) When did the Allied ground assault begin in the Gulf War?
b) How long did it last?

*Your Own Answer*_____

_____

Q348

What were the four terms for a cease-fire in the Gulf War established by the United Nations?

*Your Own Answer*_____

_____

Correct Answers

A346

a) By launching SCUD missiles into Israel
b) Iraq hoped to draw Israel into the war and break up the U.S.-Arab coalition.

A347

a) February 23, 1991
b) Four days

A348

1) Iraqi annexation of Kuwait had to be rescinded.
2) Iraq had to accept liability for damages and return Kuwaiti property.
3) Iraq had to end all military actions.
4) Iraq had to release all captives.

Questions

Q349

a) What was the estimate for the number of Iraqis killed during the war?
b) What was the estimate for the number of Americans killed?

*Your Own Answer*_____

Q350

a) When did the Communists lose their monopoly on political power in the Soviet Union?
b) What event symbolized this change?

*Your Own Answer*_____

Q351

How did the Communists attempt to regain power in August of 1991?

*Your Own Answer*_____

Correct Answers

A349

a) 100,000
b) 115

A350

a) March 13, 1991
b) A decree allowing non-Communists to run for political office

A351

They attempted a military coup to oust Gorbachev from power but it failed.

Questions

Q352

a) When did the Soviet Union officially disband?
b) What was it replaced by?

*Your Own Answer*_____

Q353

What did the 1993 START II Treaty establish?

*Your Own Answer*_____

Q354

a) When was AIDS discovered?
b) Who were its primary victims?

*Your Own Answer*_____

Correct Answers

A352

a) December 1991
b) The Commonwealth of Independent States

A353

It reduced the number of nuclear warheads for both the United States and Russia by about two thirds.

A354

a) 1981
b) Homosexual males and intravenous drug users

Questions

Q355

What new, potent illegal drug appeared in the 1980s?

Your Own Answer_____

Q356

What factors explain the drop in labor union membership in the 1980s?

Your Own Answer_____

Q357

What 1989 Supreme Court decision shifted the focus of the abortion debate from the courts to the state legislatures?

Your Own Answer_____

Correct Answers

A355

Crack cocaine

A356

The economy was shifting from heavy industry to electronics and service industries.

A357

Webster v. Reproductive Health Services, in which the Supreme Court upheld a Missouri law prohibiting public employees from performing abortions unless the mother's life was threatened

Questions

Q358

How did the recording industry respond in 1990 to conservative attacks on "indecency" in the entertainment industry?

*Your Own Answer*_____

_____

Q359

a) What precipitated the Los Angeles riots of 1991?
b) How many people died in these riots?

*Your Own Answer*_____

_____

Q360

What was the 1991 Tailhook scandal?

*Your Own Answer*_____

_____

Correct Answers

A358

By agreeing to place new uniform warning labels on recordings that contained potentially offensive language

A359

a) The acquittal of Los Angeles police officers charged in the videotaped beating of Rodney King
b) 52

A360

The scandal involved revelations that 26 women had been harassed by marine and navy fliers during a 1991 convention.

Questions

Q361

What report precipitated a crisis in education during the 1980s?

Your Own Answer_____

Q362

How did states respond to this crisis?

Your Own Answer_____

Q363

What was significant about Ross Perot's performance during the 1992 presidential election?

Your Own Answer_____

Correct Answers

A361
A 1981 report called "A Nation at Risk" prepared by the National Commission of Excellence in Education, which argued that a "rising tide of mediocrity" characterized the nation's schools

A362
Many states instituted reforms including higher teacher salaries, competency tests for teachers, and an increase in required subjects for high school graduation.

A363
Perot won 19 percent of the popular vote, which was the best performance by a candidate not nominated by the two major parties since Theodore Roosevelt in 1912.

Questions

Q364

What was the first controversy of the Clinton administration?

*Your Own Answer*_____

Q365

Explain the 1993 Family Leave Act.

*Your Own Answer*_____

Q366

Who was convicted of the 1993 World Trade Center bombing?

*Your Own Answer*_____

Correct Answers

A364

Clinton proposed to lift the ban on gays and lesbians in the military.

A365

This act required large companies to provide up to 12 weeks unpaid leave for family and medical emergencies.

A366

Four Arab terrorists

Questions

Q367

What was the 1993 "Motor-Voter" Bill?

Your Own Answer_____

Q368

a) What was the objective of the 1993 Budget Reconciliation Act?
b) How did it attempt to achieve that objective?

Your Own Answer_____

Q369

What was the 1993 National Service Act?

Your Own Answer_____

Correct Answers

A367

This bill required states to allow citizens to register to vote while applying for driver's licenses and to adopt standardized procedures for voter-registration by mail.

A368

a) To reduce the federal deficit by $496 billion by 1998
b) It combined $225 billion in spending cuts with $241 billion in new taxes over five years.

A369

This bill allowed a limited number of young people to repay federal education assistance through community service.

Questions

Q370

How many people were killed in the 1994 Los Angeles earthquake?

Your Own Answer

Q371

a) What was NAFTA?
b) Who were its most prominent critics?

Your Own Answer

Q372

What was the major provision of the 1993 Brady Bill?

Your Own Answer

Correct Answers

A370

51

A371

a) The North American Free Trade Agreement eliminated most tariffs and other trade barriers between the United States, Canada, and Mexico.
b) Organized labor and Ross Perot

A372

It established a five-day waiting period for the purchase of handguns while local law enforcement officials checked the background of prospective buyers.

Questions

Q373

What did the 1994 Crime Bill authorize?

*Your Own Answer*_____

Q374

Who did President Clinton appoint to the Supreme Court?

*Your Own Answer*_____

Q375

What was the Whitewater scandal?

*Your Own Answer*_____

Correct Answers

A373

It authorized spending $13.45 billion for state, local, and federal police with an emphasis on community policing, $9.85 billion for prisons, and $6.9 billion for crime prevention programs.

A374

Ruth Bader Ginsburg and Stephen Breyer

A375

President Clinton was criticized for wrongdoings in the Whitewater real estate developments in which he had been an investor with James B. McDougal, owner of a failed savings and loan institution, while governor of Arkansas.

Questions

Q376

What was the significance of the 1994 Congressional elections?

*Your Own Answer*_____

Q377

Who were arrested as suspects in the 1995 Oklahoma City bombing?

*Your Own Answer*_____

Q378

When did the last U.S. troops leave Somalia?

*Your Own Answer*_____

Correct Answers

A376

They gave Republicans control of both Houses of Congress for the first time since 1952.

A377

Two members of a right-wing, paramilitary militia

A378

1994

Questions

Q379

What was the result of the 1994 accord signed between Israel and the Palestinian Liberation Organization?

*Your Own Answer*_____

Q380

What was involved in the 1994 agreement between the United States and North Korea?

*Your Own Answer*_____

Q381

Why did the Clinton administration lift the trade embargo against Vietnam in 1994?

*Your Own Answer*_____

Correct Answers

A379

It established Palestinian self-rule in the Gaza Strip at Jericho.

A380

The U.S. would provide financial and technological assistance for North Korean nuclear energy in return for North Korea acepting the Nuclear Non-Proliferation Treaty.

A381

Because Vietnam cooperated with efforts to find the remains of U.S. military personnel and U.S. businesses wanted to gain access to the Vietnamese market.

Questions

Q382

Describe the 1994 immigration agreement between the United States and Cuba.

Your Own Answer

Q383

Who became the first woman to win the Nobel prize for literature in 1993?

Your Own Answer

Q384

What doctor became associated with the issue of assisted suicide for the terminally ill in the 1990s?

Your Own Answer

Correct Answers

A382

The United States agreed to allow 20,000 Cubans into the country annually in return for the Cuban government preventing its citizens from leaving Cuba in rafts and other boats for illegal entry into the U.S.

A383

Toni Morrison

A384

Dr. Jack Kevorkian

Questions

Q385

a) What significant sports event was cancelled in 1994?
b) Why?

*Your Own Answer*_____

Q386

a) What was the name of the Bull Moose Party's platform in 1912?
b) What were its major provisions?

*Your Own Answer*_____

Q387

What was the main feature of Socialist candidate Eugene Deb's platform in 1912?

*Your Own Answer*_____

Correct Answers

A385

a) The World Series
b) A player's strike

A386

a) The new nationalism
b) Federal old age; unemployment; accident insurance; eight-hour work days; woman suffrage; abolition of child labor; and expanded public health servcies

A387

A graded transition to government ownership of major industries

Questions

Q388

Who was Wilson's secretary of state in his first term?

Your Own Answer

Q389

What were the three main features of President Wilson's legislative promise in 1913?

Your Own Answer

Q390

What did the Underwood-Simmons Tariff Act of 1913 accomplish?

Your Own Answer

Correct Answers

A388

William Jennings Bryan

A389

1) Reduction of the tariff
2) Return of the banking and currency laws
3) Improvements in the anti-trust laws

A390

It reduced average rates to about 29 percent as compared with 37 percent to 40 percent under the previous Payne-Aldrich Tariff.

Questions

Q391

Describe the Adamson Act of 1916.

Your Own Answer_____

Q392

What was the name of the leading suffrage movement in the early twentieth century?

Your Own Answer_____

Q393

How did Congress respond to the immigration controversy in 1917?

Your Own Answer_____

Correct Answers

A391

This law mandated an eight-hour day for workers on interstate railroads with time and a half for overtime and a maximum of 16 hours in a shift.

A392

The National American Woman Suffrage Association

A393

Congress passed a law requiring a literacy test for immigrants.

Questions

Q394

What was the 1917 Lansing Ishii Agreement?

*Your Own Answer*_____

Q395

When did the Panama Canal open?

*Your Own Answer*_____

Q396

a) What was President Wilson's justification for sending marines into Haiti in 1915?
b) What was the result?

*Your Own Answer*_____

Correct Answers

A394

Japan recognized the Open Door in China while the United States recognized Japan's special interest in that nation.

A395

1914

A396

a) He claimed that political anarchy existed.
b) Haiti became a U.S. protectorate.

Questions

Q397

What happened in the Dominican Republic in 1916?

Your Own Answer

Q398

From what country did the U.S. purchase the Virgin Islands? When?

Your Own Answer

Q399

What was the American response when World War I broke out in Europe?

Your Own Answer

Correct Answers

A397

Wilson sent in the marines to stop a civil war and established a military government under an American naval commander.

A398

Denmark in 1916

A399

President Wilson issued a proclamation of American neutrality on August 4, 1914.

Questions

Q400

a) What was the Gore-McLemore Resolution?
b) What happened to it?

*Your Own Answer*_____

Q401

What did the National Defense Act of 1916 do?

*Your Own Answer*_____

Q402

When did the United States declare war against Germany?

*Your Own Answer*_____

Correct Answers

A400

a) It would have prohibited American travel on armed ships or on ships carrying munitions.
b) It was defeated in Congress after intense lobbying by Wilson.

A401

It increased the army from 90,000 to 220,000 and enlarged the National Guard under federal control.

A402

April 6, 1917

Questions

Q403

What was the primary role of blacks in the army during World War I?

*Your Own Answer*_____

Q404

When did Americans experience their first important military engagements in World War I?

*Your Own Answer*_____

Q405

What was the Fuel Administration?

*Your Own Answer*_____

Correct Answers

A403
They were kept in segregated units, usually with white officers, which were used as labor battalions or for other support activites. Some black units, however, did see combat.

A404
The spring of 1918

A405
Established in 1917, it was concerned primarily with coal production and conservation because coal was the predominant fuel of the time.

Questions

Q406

What did the U.S. Railroad Administration do?

*Your Own Answer*_____

Q407

Why was the Emergency Fleet Corporation created in 1917?

*Your Own Answer*_____

Q408

What did the Revenue Act of 1918 do?

*Your Own Answer*_____

Correct Answers

A406

It took over and operated all the railroads in the country as one system. The government paid the owners rent for the use of their land and spent over $500 million for improved trucks and equipment.

A407

To buy, build, lease, and operate merchant ships for the war effort

A408

It imposed a personal income tax of six percent on incomes up to $4,000 and 12 percent on incomes above that amount.

Questions

Q409

Who was responsible for defeating the suffrage amendment in 1918?

Your Own Answer

Q410

How did the war affect the Prohibition movement?

Your Own Answer

Q411

How did the Bolshevik Revolution affect the Versailles Conference?

Your Own Answer

Correct Answers

A409

Southern farmers in the senate

A410

Proponents of Prohibition stressed the need for military personnel to be sober and the need to conserve grain for food.

A411

The threat of international Communism resulted in the Western powers remaining united after the war.

Questions

Q412

When did Prohibition become effective?

*Your Own Answer*_____

Q413

What was the Seattle General Strike about?

*Your Own Answer*_____

Q414

a) Why did coal workers strike in 1919?
b) How was the issue resolved?

*Your Own Answer*_____

Correct Answers

A412

January 1920

A413

In January 1919, all unions in Seattle declared a general strike in support of a strike for higher pay by shipyard workers. The action was widely condemned, the federal government sent marines, and the strike was soon abandoned.

A414

a) For shorter hours and higher wages
b) Attorney General Mitchell Palmer obtained injunctions and the union called off the strike. An arbitration board later awarded the miners a wage increase.

Questions

Q415

What was the major planks of the Republican platform in 1920?

Your Own Answer

Q416

What was a major factor behind the recession of the 1920s?

Your Own Answer

Q417

What was the major reason for the improved economy during most of the 1920s?

Your Own Answer

Correct Answers

A415

Opposition to the League of Nations, low taxes, high tariffs, immigration restriction, and aid to farmers

A416

Europe returned to normal and reduced its purchases in America and domestic demand for goods not available in wartime was filled. Prices fell and unemployment exceeded 12 percent in 1921.

A417

Improved industrial efficiency which resulted in lower prices for goods

Questions

Q418

What was the price of a Ford Model T in 1925?

*Your Own Answer*_____

Q419

What spurred consumer interest and demand in the 1920s?

*Your Own Answer*_____

Q420

Why did the demand for business loans decline in the 1920s?

*Your Own Answer*_____

Correct Answers

A418

$290

A419

A great increase in professional advertising using newspapers, magazines, radio, billboards, and other media

A420

Because corporations were raising much of their money through the sale of stocks and bonds

Questions

Q421

What industries witnessed the most violent labor confrontations during the 1920s?

*Your Own Answer*_____

Q422

What was the American population by 1930?

*Your Own Answer*_____

Q423

What was the first year that a majority of Americans lived in urban areas?

*Your Own Answer*_____

Correct Answers

A421

Mining and southern textile industries

A422

Roughly 123 million

A423

1920

Questions

Q424

How did the sexual revolution affect women's clothing in the 1920s?

Your Own Answer

Q425

What two popular forms of music were developed during the 1920s, primarily by black musicians?

Your Own Answer

Q426

What did the Smith-Hughes Act of 1917 do?

Your Own Answer

Correct Answers

A424

Women adopted less bulky clothing, wearing short skirts and sleeveless and low-cut dresses.

A425

Jazz and blues

A426

Gave federal funds for agricultural and technical studies

Questions

Q427

What was the only issue which united most Protestants in the 1920s?

Your Own Answer____

Q428

a) When was sound introduced to motion pictures?
b) In what movie?

Your Own Answer____

Q429

What event contributed to the decline of the Ku Klux Klan after 1925?

Your Own Answer____

Correct Answers

A427

Support for Prohibition

A428

a) 1927
b) *The Jazz Singer*

A429

The murder conviction of Indiana Grand Dragon David Stephenson

Questions

Q430

Who was the most famous bootlegging gangster?

Your Own Answer

Q431

Who was President Harding's secretary of state?

Your Own Answer

Q432

What was the major plank of the Republican Party platform in 1924?

Your Own Answer

Correct Answers

A430

Al Capone

A431

Charles Evans Hughes

A432

The party stood on its record of economic growth and prosperity since 1922.

Questions

Q433

What was the major thrust of the Progressive Party platform in 1924?

*Your Own Answer*_____

Q434

What Veterans legislation was passed in 1924?

*Your Own Answer*_____

Q435

Name the Nicaraguan revolutionary figure who was the reason American marines were returned to the country in 1925.

*Your Own Answer*_____

Correct Answers

A433

The platform attacked monopolies, and called for the nationalization of railroads and the direct election of the president.

A434

Legislation was passed to give veterans of World War I 20-year endowment policies with values based on their length of service.

A435

General Augusto Sandino was the forerunner of the movement which would eventually become Sandinistas.

Questions

Q436

Describe President Hoover's economic philosophy.

Your Own Answer_____

Q437

What were "Hoovervilles"?

Your Own Answer_____

Q438

What was the Federal Home Loan Bank Act of 1932?

Your Own Answer_____

Correct Answers

A436

He believed that an economic system with voluntary cooperation of business and government would enable the United States to abolish poverty through continued economic growth.

A437

Makeshift shacks which housed hundreds of thousands of homeless people in empty spaces around cities during the Depression

A438

This law created home loan banks with a capital of $125 million to make loans to building and loan assocations, savings banks, and insurance companies to help them avoid foreclosure on homes.

Questions

Q439

On what ballot was Franklin D. Roosevelt nominated by the Democratic party in 1932?

Your Own Answer

Q440

Who was the first woman appointed to a cabinet position?

Your Own Answer

Q441

What happened during the first hundred days of the Roosevelt administration?

Your Own Answer

Correct Answers

A439

Fourth ballot

A440

Frances Perkins was appointed secretary of labor by FDR in 1933.

A441

The basic economic recovery plan of the Roosevelt administration was passed by Congress.

Questions

Q442

What was the objective of the Agricultural Adjustment Act of 1933?

*Your Own Answer*_____

Q443

What was the effect of the first New Deal policies on unemployment?

*Your Own Answer*_____

Q444

a) When was the American Liberty League formed?
b) What was its objective?
c) Who was its principal financer?

*Your Own Answer*_____

Correct Answers

A442

It sought to return farm prices to parity with those of the 1909 to 1914 period.

A443

Unemployment dropped from about 25 percent of nonfarm workers in 1933 to about 20 percent in 1935 but this was still much higher than the 3.2 percent of pre-depression 1929.

A444

a) 1934
b) To defend business interests and promote the open shop
c) The DuPont family

Questions

Q445

Who founded the Share Our Wealth Society in 1934?

*Your Own Answer*_____

Q446

Who was the leader of the National Union for Social Justice?

*Your Own Answer*_____

Q447

What did the National Youth Administration do?

*Your Own Answer*_____

Correct Answers

A445

Senator Huey Long of Louisiana

A446

Father Charles E. Coughlin

A447

It provided part-time jobs for high school and college students to enable them to stay in school and to help young adults not in school to find jobs.

Questions

Q448

a) What was the aim of the Resettlement Administration (RA)?
b) When was it created?

Your Own Answer

Q449

What was the Wheeler-Rayburn Act of 1935?

Your Own Answer

Q450

What did the Motor Carrier Act of 1935 do?

Your Own Answer

Correct Answers

A448

a) It relocated destitute families from seemingly hopeless situations to new rural homestead communities or to suburban greenbelt towns.
b) 1935

A449

It empowered the Securities and Exchange Commission to restrict public utility holding companies to one natural region and to eliminate duplicate holding companies.

A450

It extended the regulatory authority of the Interstate Commerce Commission to cover interstate trucking lines.

Questions

Q451

What were the main features of the Democratic platform of 1936?

*Your Own Answer*_____

Q452

What was the Republican ticket in the 1936 presidential election?

*Your Own Answer*_____

Q453

What was the result of the Bankhead-Jones Farm Tenancy Act passed in July 1937?

*Your Own Answer*_____

Correct Answers

A451

The platform promised an expanded farm program, labor legislation, more rural electrification, and public housing and enforcement of the antitrust laws.

A452

Alf Landon and Frank Knox

A453

The result was creation of the Farm Security Administration (FSA) to replace the Resettlement Administration. The FSA continued the homestead projects, and loaned money to farmers to purchase farms, lease land, and buy equipment.

Questions

Q454

Explain the Second Agricultural Adjustment Act of February 1938.

Your Own Answer

Q455

What was the most popular form of music in the 1930s?

Your Own Answer

Q456

What happened at the Montevideo Conference in 1933?

Your Own Answer

Correct Answers

A454

This act appropriated funds for soil conservation payments to farmers who would remove land from production.

A455

Swing or big band music

A456

The United States renamed the right of intervention in the internal affairs of Latin American countries and also agreed to submit all American disputes to arbitration.

Questions

Q457

a) What was the aim of the London Economic Conference in 1933?
b) Why did it fail?

*Your Own Answer*_____

Q458

What did the Tydings-McDuffie Act of 1934 accomplish?

*Your Own Answer*_____

Q459

What senator let the investigation of profiteering by bankers and munitions makers in drawing the United States into World War I?

*Your Own Answer*_____

Correct Answers

A457

a) To obtain tariff reduction and currency stabilization for the industrialized nations
b) Lack of American cooperation

A458

It forced the Phillipines to become independent on July 4, 1946 rather than grant dominion status which the Phillipines had requested.

A459

Senator Gerald Nye of North Dakota

Questions

Q460

What did the Neutrality Acts of 1936 do?

Your Own Answer

Q461

a) What famous foreign policy speech did President Roosevelt give in 1937?
b) How did the public respond?

Your Own Answer

Q462

What were the main provisions of the Neutrality Act of 1939?

Your Own Answer

Correct Answers

A460

The laws gave the president authority to determine when a state of war existed, and prohibited any loans or credits to belligerents.

A461

a) He gave the "Quarantine the Agressor" speech, in which he proposed that the democracies unite to quarantine the agressor nations.
b) When public opinion did not pick up the idea, he did not press the issue.

A462

It allowed the cash-and-carry sale of arms and short-term loans to belligerents, but forbade American ships to trade with belligerents or Americans to trade on belligerent ships.

Questions

Q463

a) What was the purpose of the Council on National Defense?
b) Who was its first chairman?

Your Own Answer_____

Q464

Who was Roosevelt's controversial choice for vice president in 1940?

Your Own Answer_____

Q465

a) When did the United States occupy Iceland?
b) Why?

Your Own Answer_____

Correct Answers

A463

a) To direct defense production and especially to build fifty thousand planes
b) William Knudson, president of General Motors

A464

Secretary of Agriculture Henry A. Wallace

A465

a) July 1941
b) To protect it from seizure by Germany

Questions

Q466

What was the Greater East Asia Co-Prosperity sphere?

Your Own Answer

Q467

What did the 1940 embargo against Japan involve?

Your Own Answer

Q468

What was the American condition regarding holding a summit conference with Japan in August 1941?

Your Own Answer

Correct Answers

A466

It was the Japanese term for their goal of an empire of undefined boundaries in east Asia and the western Pacific.

A467

The embargo involved the export of aviator gasoline, lubricants, and scrap iron. In December, the embargo was extended to include iron ore and pig iron, some chemicals, and machine tools.

A468

Japan had to agree to leave China first, which it did not do.

Questions

Q469

When did Germany invade the Soviet Union?

Your Own Answer

Q470

How did Congress respond to the sinking of the *Reuben James*?

Your Own Answer

Q471

What did the Declaration of the United Nations establish?

Your Own Answer

Correct Answers

A469

June 1941

A470

By authorizing the arming of American merchant ships and permitting them to carry cargo to Allied ports

A471

On January 1, 1942, 26 nations pledged themselves to the principles of the Atlantic Charter and promised not to make a separate peace with their common enemies.

Questions

Q472

a) When was the War Production Board established?
b) What was its purpose?

*Your Own Answer*_____

Q473

What was the result of the Reserve Act of 1942?

*Your Own Answer*_____

Q474

Who was the Republican nominee for president in 1949?

*Your Own Answer*_____

Correct Answers

A472

a) 1942
b) To regulate the use of raw materials

A473

To extend the income tax to the majority of the population

A474

New York Governor Thomas Dewey

Questions

Q475

When did the Allied army attack French North Africa?

Your Own Answer

Q476

When did Rommel's Africa Korps surrender?

Your Own Answer

Q477

When was Paris liberated by Allied armies?

Your Own Answer

Correct Answers

A475

November 1942

A476

May 1943

A477

August 1944

Questions

Q478

When did Germany surrender?

*Your Own Answer*_____

Q479

a) When was Manila liberated?
b) What general led the forces?

*Your Own Answer*_____

Q480

What scientist is credited with producing the first atomic chain reaction?

*Your Own Answer*_____

Correct Answers

A478

May 7, 1945

A479

a) March 1945
b) General Douglas McArthur

A480

Enrico Fermi of the University of Chicago

Questions

Q481

What was the name of the plane that dropped the atomic bomb on Hiroshima?

*Your Own Answer*_____

_____

Q482

When did the Soviet Union enter the war against Japan?

*Your Own Answer*_____

_____

Q483

When was the second atomic bomb dropped on Nagasaki?

*Your Own Answer*_____

_____

Correct Answers

A481

The Enola Gay

A482

August 8, 1945

A483

August 9, 1945

Questions

Q484

During what two year period did the Soviet Union take over Poland, Hungary, Rumania, and Bulgaria?

Your Own Answer

Q485

a) What Soviet action prompted the Berlin Crisis in June 1948?
b) How did the United States respond?

Your Own Answer

Q486

When did the Soviets explode their first atomic device?

Your Own Answer

Correct Answers

A484

1946–47

A485

a) The Soviets blocked surface access to Berlin.
b) The U.S. instituted an airlift to transport supplies to the city until the Soviets lifted their blockade in May 1949.

A486

September 1949

Questions

Q487

What countries were named to be permanent members of the United Nations Security Council?

Your Own Answer

Q488

Who was the leader of the Nationalist Chinese government on Taiwan?

Your Own Answer

Q489

When did North Korea invade South Korea?

Your Own Answer

Correct Answers

A487

The United States, Great Britian, France, the Soviet Union, and China

A488

Chiang Kai-shek

A489

June 1950

Questions

Q490

a) When was the Southeast Asia Treaty Organization formed?
b) What Asian countries joined?

Your Own Answer

Q491

How did President Eisenhower respond to the shelling of the nationalist occupied island of Quemoy and Matsu by the Communist Chinese?

Your Own Answer

Q492

a) What countries participated in the Summit Conference of 1955?
b) What subjects were discussed?

Your Own Answer

Correct Answers

A490

a) September 1954
b) Phillipines, Thailand and Pakistan

A491

He obtained authorization from Congress to defend Formosa (Taiwan) and related areas

A492

a) United States, Great Britan, France and the Soviet Union
b) Disarmament and the reunification of Germany

Questions

Q493

From what state was Harry Truman a senator before he became president?

Your Own Answer_____

Q494

a) When did President Truman end most price controls?
b) What three items were exempted from this move?

Your Own Answer_____

Q495

Who was the leader of the United Mine Workers?

Your Own Answer_____

Correct Answers

A493

Missouri

A494

a) 1946
b) Rents, sugar, and rice

A495

John L. Lewis

Questions

Q496

What did the Organization Act of 1949 establish?

Your Own Answer

Q497

What civil rights measures did President Truman enact in 1948?

Your Own Answer

Q498

What did the Presidential Succession Act of 1947 do?

Your Own Answer

Correct Answers

A496

It allowed the president to make organizational changes subject to congressional veto.

A497

He banned racial discrimination in federal government hiring practices and ordered the desegregation of the armed forces.

A498

It placed the speaker of the house and the president pro tempore of the Senate ahead of the secretary of state and after the vice president in the line of succession.

Questions

Q499

What speech propelled Senator Joseph McCarthy of Wisconsin into national prominence?

Your Own Answer

Q500

How did President Eisenhower describe his legislative program?

Your Own Answer

Q501

What was the minimum wage in 1955?

Your Own Answer

Correct Answers

A499

During a February 9, 1950 speech, McCarthy stated that he had a list of known Communists who were working in the State Department.

A500

"Dynamic Conservatism"

A501

$1.00 an hour

Questions

Q502

a) Who was the Democratic nominee for president in 1956?
b) How many states did he carry?

*Your Own Answer*_____

Q503

Why did White House Chief of Staff Sherman Adams have to resign in 1958?

*Your Own Answer*_____

Q504

What two Supreme Court decisions stipulated that blacks must be allowed to attend integrated law schools?

*Your Own Answer*_____

Correct Answers

A502

a) Alan Stevenson
b) Seven

A503

It was revealed that he had received gifts in return for helping a Boston industrialist deal with the federal bureaucracy.

A504

Ada Lois Sipuel v. Board of Regents (1948) and *Sweatt v. Painter* (1950)

Questions

Q505

What was the White Citizens Council?

*Your Own Answer*_____

Q506

What happened in Little Rock in 1957 concerning race relations?

*Your Own Answer*_____

Q507

What is Rosa Parks famous for?

*Your Own Answer*_____

Correct Answers

A505

It was the leading organization throughout the South in resisting the *Brown v. Board of Education* decision.

A506

Eisenhower sent 10,000 National Guardsmen and 1,000 paratroopers to control mobs and enable blacks to enroll in Central High.

A507

Her arrest on December 11, 1955 was a catalyst for the civil rights movement. She was arrested for refusing to give up her seat on a bus to a white passenger.

Questions

Q508

How did John F. Kennedy defuse the issue of his Catholicism during the 1960 campaign?

Your Own Answer

Q509

What was Kennedy's margin of victory in the popular vote in the 1960 election?

Your Own Answer

Q510

How much did home ownership grow by between 1945 and 1960?

Your Own Answer

Correct Answers

A508

He told a gathering of Protestant ministers that he accepted separation of church and state and that Catholic leaders would not tell him how to act as president.

A509

Slightly over 100,000 votes

A510

50 percent

Questions

Q511

Who became an increasingly important consumer group during the 1950s?

*Your Own Answer*_____

Q512

How did the Federal Housing Administration contribute to increased home ownership?

*Your Own Answer*_____

Q513

What happened to the work week during the 1950s?

*Your Own Answer*_____

Correct Answers

A511

Teenagers

A512

It helped builders by insuring up to 95 percent of a loan and buyers by insuring their mortgages.

A513

It shrank from six to five days.

Questions

Q514

Why did President Kennedy send the National Guard into Mississippi in the fall of 1962?

*Your Own Answer*_____

Q515

When was the Berlin Wall erected?

*Your Own Answer*_____

Q516

What important economic legislation was passed by Congress in 1964?

*Your Own Answer*_____

Correct Answers

A514

To ensure that a black student, James Meredith, could enroll at the University of Mississippi

A515

1961

A516

A $10 billion tax cut

Questions

Q517

Who did President Johnson defeat in the presidential election of 1964?

*Your Own Answer*_____

Q518

What new federal department was established in 1966?

*Your Own Answer*_____

Q519

a) Who were the first men to walk on the moon?
b) When?

*Your Own Answer*_____

Correct Answers

A517

He defeated Republican nominee Senator Barry Goldwater from Arizona.

A518

The Department of Housing and Urban Affairs

A519

a) Neil Armstrong and Edwin Aldrin
b) July 20, 1969

Questions

Q520

What did the Voting Rights Act of 1965 authorize?

Your Own Answer

Q521

How many people were killed in the riots in Watts in 1965?

Your Own Answer

Q522

Who were the two leading figures in the Black Power movement during the 1960s?

Your Own Answer

Correct Answers

A520

It authorized the attorney gerneral to appoint officials to register voters.

A521

34

A522

Stokely Carmichael and H. Rap Brown

Questions

Q523

What was a common criticism of universities by student protesters during the 1960s?

*Your Own Answer*_____

Q524

What split the anti-war movement during the 1960s?

*Your Own Answer*_____

Q525

What was the class origins of the women's movement?

*Your Own Answer*_____

Correct Answers

A523

The common criticism was bureaucracies were indifferent to student needs.

A524

It split between those favoring violence and those opposed to it.

A525

The women's movement was largely limited to the middle class.

Questions

Q526

What encouraged freer sexual practices during the 1960s?

*Your Own Answer*_____

Q527

What event was a catalyst for the gay rights movement?

*Your Own Answer*_____

Q528

How many American troops were in Vietnam by 1968?

*Your Own Answer*_____

Correct Answers

A526

New methods of birth control, particularly the "pill"

A527

A police raid in 1969 on the Stonewall Inn, a gay hangout in Greenwich Village

A528

538,000

Questions

Q529

Who led the 1966 Congressional investigations of the Vietnam War?

*Your Own Answer*_____

Q530

Who did Richard Nixon choose as his running mate in 1968?

*Your Own Answer*_____

Q531

Who were the two Supreme Court nominees of President Nixon defeated in the Senate?

*Your Own Answer*_____

Correct Answers

A529

Senator J. William Fulbright

A530

Spiro Agnew

A531

Clement Haynesworth and G. Harrold Carswell

Questions

Q532

a) What was President Nixon's proposal to reform welfare?
b) What happened to it?

Your Own Answer

Q533

What happened at My Lai?

Your Own Answer

Q534

Why did President Nixon resume bombing of North Vietnam in December of 1972?

Your Own Answer

Correct Answers

A532

a) He proposed that the bulk of payments be shifted to the states and that a "minimum income" be established for poor families.
b) The proposal didn't pass Congress.

A533

An American massacre of the Vietnamese

A534

Nixon claimed that the North Vietnamese were not bargaining in good faith.

Questions

Q535

Why did Senator Thomas Eagleton resign as Democratic vice president nominee in 1972?

*Your Own Answer*_____

Q536

When was George Wallace shot?

*Your Own Answer*_____

Q537

Whose testimony implicated President Nixon in the Watergate coverup?

*Your Own Answer*_____

Correct Answers

A535

The press revealed that Eagleton had previously been treated for psychological problems.

A536

May 15, 1972

A537

John Dean

Questions

Q538

What three articles of impeachment were adopted by the House Judiciary Committee against President Nixon?

Your Own Answer_____

Q539

What was the name of President Ford's anti-inflation compaign?

Your Own Answer_____

Q540

In what year did New York City verge on bankruptcy?

Your Own Answer_____

Correct Answers

A538

It charged the president with obstructing justice, misusing presidential power, and failing to obey the committee's subpoenas

A539

WIN-WHIP Inflation Now

A540

1975

Questions

Q541

Which president offered amnesty to Americans who had fled the draft and gone to other countries during the Vietnam War?

Your Own Answer

Q542

What was the basis of President Carter's foreign policy?

Your Own Answer

Q543

Who did Ronald Reagan pick as his Republican running mate in 1980?

Your Own Answer

Correct Answers

A541

President Carter

A542

Human rights considerations

A543

George Bush

Questions

Q544

What major change happened in the 1980 congressional elections?

Your Own Answer_____

Q545

What was the median age for Americans in 1980?

Your Own Answer_____

Q546

What was the political tendency of the "Sunbelt" states during the 1980s?

Your Own Answer_____

Correct Answers

A544

The Republicans took control of the Senate.

A545

30

A546

Conservative

Questions

Q547

What popular 1973 movie examined the end of 1950s style innocence?

*Your Own Answer*_____

Q548

What was the cause of the 1982 recession?

*Your Own Answer*_____

Q549

What 1982 legislation reversed some of the concessions made to business in 1981?

*Your Own Answer*_____

Correct Answers

A547

American Graffiti

A548

The Federal Reserve's "tight money" policy

A549

The Tax Equity and Fiscal Responsibility Act

Questions

Q550

What anti-union measure did President Reagan make in 1981?

Your Own Answer_____

Q551

What was President Reagan's term to describe the Soviet Union?

Your Own Answer_____

Q552

How did the United States support the forces opposed to the Sandinista regime in Nicaragua?

Your Own Answer_____

Correct Answers

A550

He fired all striking air traffic controllers.

A551

"Evil Empire"

A552

With arms, tactical supports, and intelligence

Questions

Q553

What is the only part of the Democratic coalition that supported Mondale's 1989 candidacy?

*Your Own Answer*_____

Q554

What country did the United States launch an air strike against in 1986 in retaliation for alleged terrorism?

*Your Own Answer*_____

Q555

What was the Iran-Contra scandal all about?

*Your Own Answer*_____

Correct Answers

A553

Black Americans

A554

Libya

A555

It was revealed that the United States had sold arms to Iranians in hopes of encouraging them to use their influence to get American hostages in Lebanon released. The profits from these sales were then diverted to the Nicaraguan contras in an attempt to get around congressional restrictions on funding the countries.

Questions

Q556

In what year did the Sandinistas and the contras agree to cease-fire?

Your Own Answer_____

Q557

How did Congress respond to the fears of the recession in November 1987?

Your Own Answer_____

Q558

What three new appointments did President Reagan make to the Supreme Court?

Your Own Answer_____

Correct Answers

A556

1988

A557

It reduced 1988 taxes by $30 billion.

A558

Sandra Day O'Connor, Antonin Scalia, and Anthony Kennedy

Questions

Q559

What eliminated Senator Gary Hart from the 1988 presidential race?

Your Own Answer_____

Q560

Who did Michael Dukakis select as his running mate in 1988?

Your Own Answer_____

Q561

What were the major themes of George Bush's presidential campaign in 1988?

Your Own Answer_____

Correct Answers

A559

A sex scandal

A560

Senator Lloyd Bentsen of Texas

A561

Patriotism, defense, anti-crime, and anti-taxes

Questions

Q562

What was the recommendation of 1989 Commission of Base Realignment and Closure?

*Your Own Answer*_____

Q563

What was the only sector of the economy not to experience an economic slowdown in the late 1980s?

*Your Own Answer*_____

Q564

What senior citizen lobbying group became influential during the 1980s?

*Your Own Answer*_____

Correct Answers

A562

The closing of 54 military bases

A563

Medical services

A564

American Association of Retired Persons (AARP)

Questions

Q565

What event led to Hungary breaking away from the Communist bloc?

*Your Own Answer*_____

Q566

When did German reunification take place?

*Your Own Answer*_____

Q567

Who was the Romanian dictator killed by anti-communist protesters on Christmas Day 1989?

*Your Own Answer*_____

Correct Answers

A565

In August 1989, Hungary opened its borders with Austria.

A566

October 1990

A567

Nicolae Ceausescu

Questions

Q568

At what summit did President Bush and Mikhail Gorbachev pronounce an end to the Cold War?

*Your Own Answer*_____

Q569

How did the United States encourage Egypt to support its position during the Persian Gulf crisis?

*Your Own Answer*_____

Q570

When did Congress authorize the urge of force during the Gulf War?

*Your Own Answer*_____

Correct Answers

A568

At Malta, in December of 1989

A569

It forgave Egypt its debt to the United States.

A570

January 12, 1991

Questions

Q571

Who was the commander of the U.S. forces in the Gulf War?

Your Own Answer

Q572

a) What kind of weapons were especially utilized during the Gulf War?
b) Provide examples.

Your Own Answer

Q573

When was a permanent cease-fire established in the Gulf War?

Your Own Answer

Correct Answers

A571

Army General H. Norman Schwarzkopf

A572

a) High technology
b) Stealth fighter, Tomahawk cruise missiles, and Patriot anti-missile missiles

A573

April 3, 1991

Questions

Q574

a) What were the three United States post-war goals for the Middle East?
b) At what conference were these goals announced?

Your Own Answer

Q575

When did Lithuania declare its independence of the Soviet Union?

Your Own Answer

Q576

What arms control initiative did President Bush announce in September of 1991?

Your Own Answer

Correct Answers

A574

a) Regional arm control and security arrangements; international aid for reconstruction of Iraq and Kuwait; and the resolution of the Israeli-Palestinian conflict
b) Middle East Conference at Madrid, Spain in October 1991

A575

March 11, 1990

A576

The unilateral removal and destruction of ground based nuclear weapons in Europe and Asia.

Questions

Q577

What popular television preacher was involved in a sex and money scandal in 1987?

*Your Own Answer*_____

Q578

What contributed to the growing number of illegitimate births in the United States in the 1980s?

*Your Own Answer*_____

Q579

Who did President Bush appoint as "Drug Czar" in 1989?

*Your Own Answer*_____

Correct Answers

A577

Jim Bakker

A578

The increased number of couples living together without getting married

A579

William Bennett

Questions

Q580

What was the name of the militant anti-abortion group that became active during the early 1990s?

*Your Own Answer*_____

_____

Q581

What was the thesis of Kevin Phillip's influential 1990 book *The Politics of Rich and Poor*?

*Your Own Answer*_____

_____

Q582

What controversy surrounded the National Endowment for the Arts in 1989?

*Your Own Answer*_____

_____

Correct Answers

A580

Operation Rescue

A581

That the economic policies of the 1980s resulted in a greater gap between the rich and the poor in the United States.

A582

That it was using federal money to support "obscene or indecent projects"

Questions

Q583

What two popular films of the late 1980s examined the Vietnam War?

Your Own Answer

Q584

Who challenged George Bush for the Republican nomination in 1982?

Your Own Answer

Q585

What were the major campaign themes emphasized by Bill Clinton in 1992?

Your Own Answer

Correct Answers

A583

Platoon and *Born on the Fourth of July*

A584

Conservative columnist Patrick Buchanan

A585

Economic issues particularly the deficit and the need to create more jobs

Questions

Q586

What percentage of the popular vote was won by Bill Clinton in 1992?

Your Own Answer

Q587

What restriction on abortion was lifted by the Clinton administration in January of 1993?

Your Own Answer

Q588

a) What event started the Waco crisis in 1993?
b) How did the crisis end?

Your Own Answer

Correct Answers

A586

43 percent

A587

The "Gag Rule," which forbid discussion of abortion with patients at federally funded family planning clinics

A588

a) In February 1993, the U.S. Bureau of Alcohol, Tobacco and Firearms raided the headquarters of the Branch Davidian religious cult near Waco, Texas, resulting in the killing of four federal agents.

b) After a 51 day stand off, the F.B.I. attacked the compound with tear gas and began destroying walls of the compound. Cult members apparently started a fire, resulting in the deaths of 72 Branch Davidians including their leader David Koresh.

Questions

Q589

In 1994, how did the Federal Reserve respond to the fears of increased inflation?

Your Own Answer_____

Q590

a) What were the main components of the Clinton administration's health care reform plan?
b) Who were the plan's major opponents?

Your Own Answer_____

Q591

What were the major campaign themes of the Republicans during the 1994 congressional elections?

Your Own Answer_____

Correct Answers

A589

By beginning a series of interest rate increases

A590

a) Universal coverage with a guaranteed benefits package and managed competition through health care alliances which would bargain with insurance companies.
b) Republicans, small businesses, and insurance and medical-business interests.

A591

Opposition to big government and taxes

Questions

Q592

Why were American troops sent to Haiti in 1994?

Your Own Answer_____

Q593

What did NATO offer former Warsaw Pact countries in 1994?

Your Own Answer_____

Q594

Why was there strong opposition to the Clinton administration's decision to continue China's "Most Favored Nation" trading status?

Your Own Answer_____

Correct Answers

A592

To ensure social stability during the period of transition from the military regime to the popularly elected Aristide government

A593

Limited association to enhance European security

A594

Because of the lack of improvements in political freedom in that country

Questions

Q595

Why did President Clinton order American troops into the Persian Gulf in October of 1994?

Your Own Answer_____

_____

Q596

Who directed these two controversial political films in the early 1990s?
a) *JFK*
b) *Malcom X*

Your Own Answer_____

_____

Q597

What is an explanation for the return of many "Baby Boomers" to churches during the 1990s?

Your Own Answer_____

_____

Correct Answers

A595

It was in response to an Iraqi military buildup on its border with Kuwait.

A596

a) Oliver Stone
b) Spike Lee

A597

The increased family responsibilities of this group

Questions

Q598

What controversies surrounded the Catholic church during the 1990s in the United States?

*Your Own Answer*_____

Q599

How did the FDA respond in 1994 to the growing concern over the negative effects of dietary fat?

*Your Own Answer*_____

Q600

a) What was the unemployment rate at the end of 1993?
b) Why was that significant?

*Your Own Answer*_____

Correct Answers

A598

1) Women in the priesthood
2) Celibacy of priests
3) Birth control
4) Abortion

A599

By requiring food manufacturers to use new labeling on the packaged foods, which gave the percentage of their daily recommended amounts per serving for various substances including fats.

A600

a) 64 percent
b) It was the lowest rate since January of 1991.

BLANK CARDS
To Make Up Your Own Questions

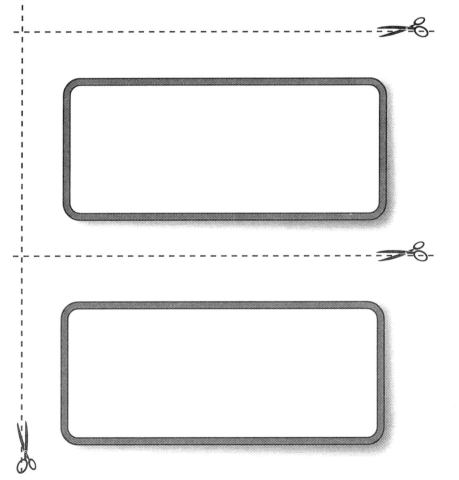

CORRECT ANSWERS
for
Your Own Questions

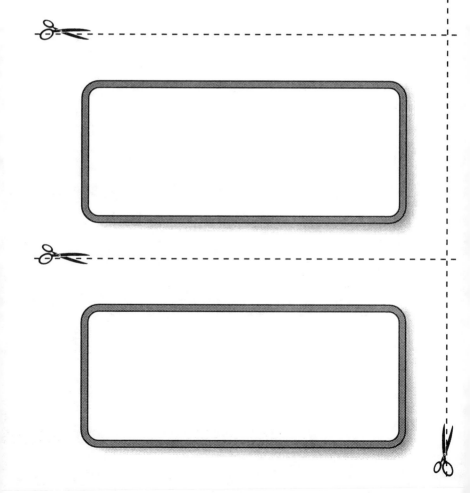

Blank Cards for
Your Own Questions

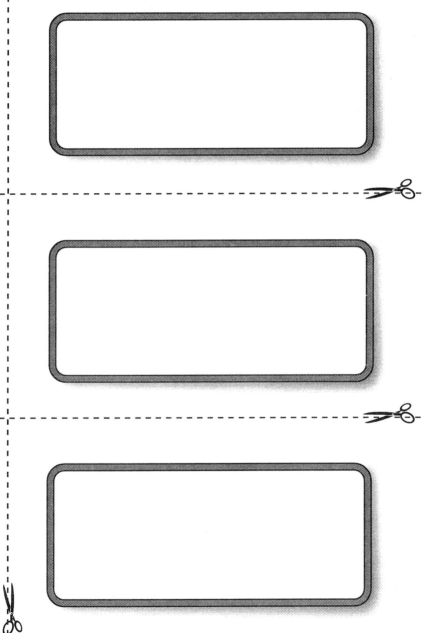

Correct Answers

Blank Cards for
Your Own Questions

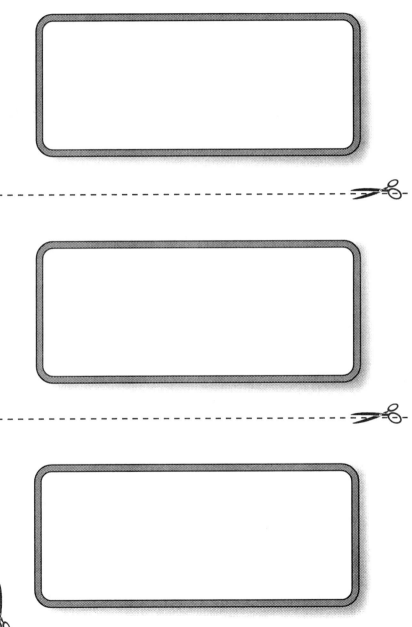

Correct Answers

Blank Cards for *Your Own Questions*

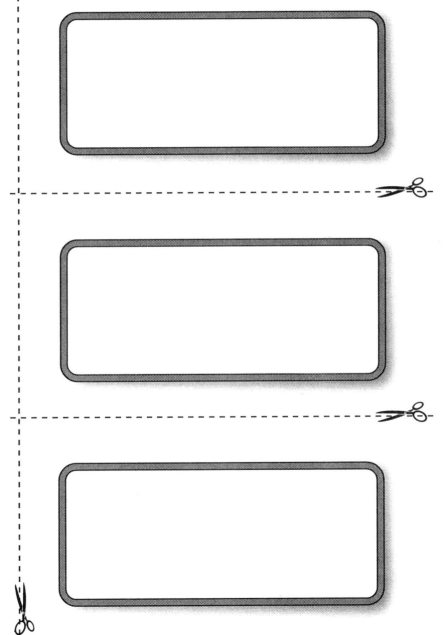

Correct Answers

Blank Cards for *Your Own Questions*

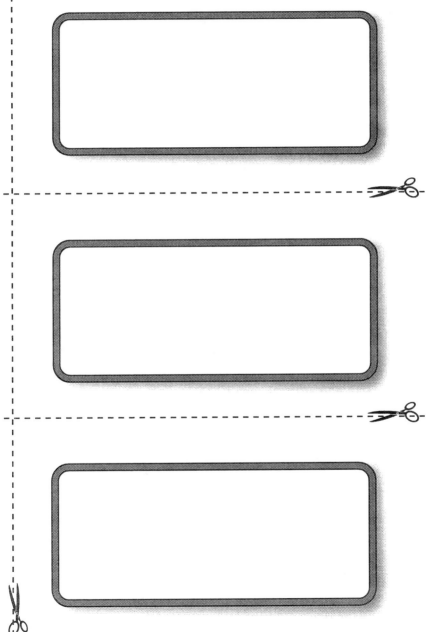

Correct Answers

Blank Cards for
Your Own Questions

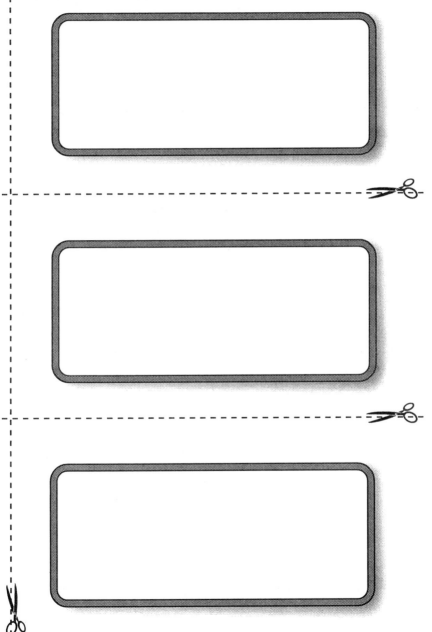

Correct Answers

Blank Cards for
Your Own Questions

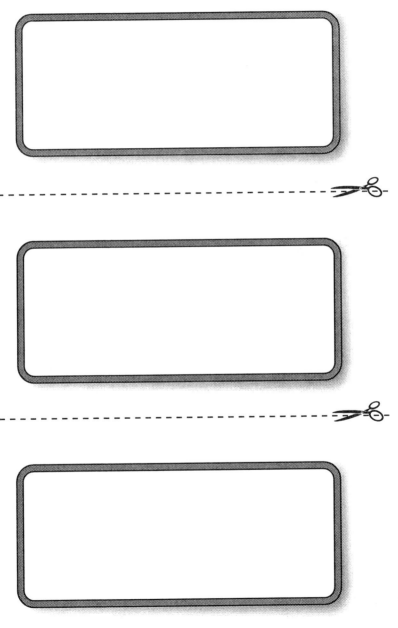

Correct Answers

Blank Cards for *Your Own Questions*

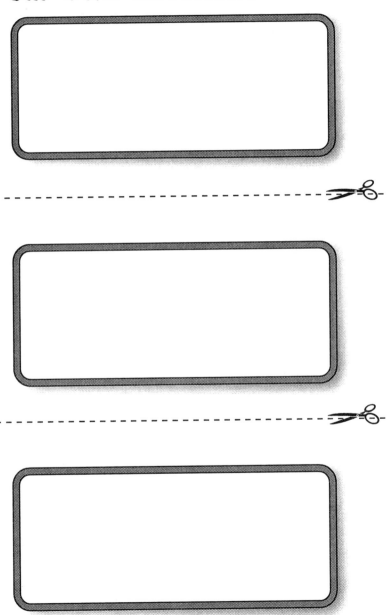

Correct Answers

Blank Cards for *Your Own Questions*

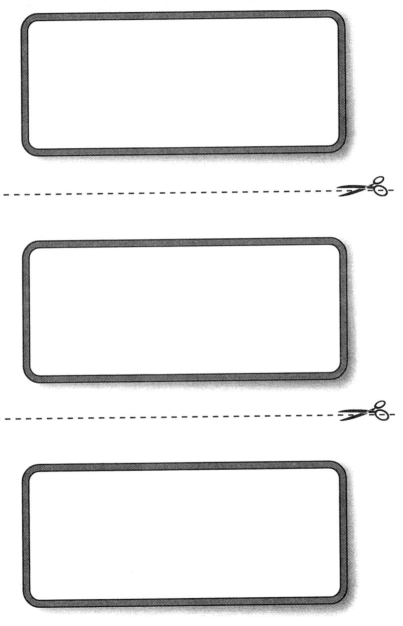

Correct Answers

Blank Cards for *Your Own Questions*

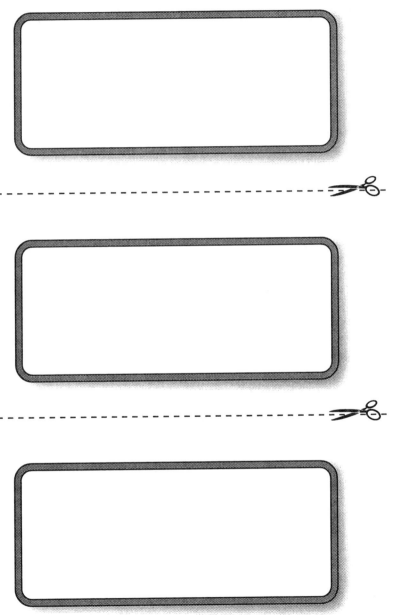

Correct Answers

Blank Cards for *Your Own Questions*

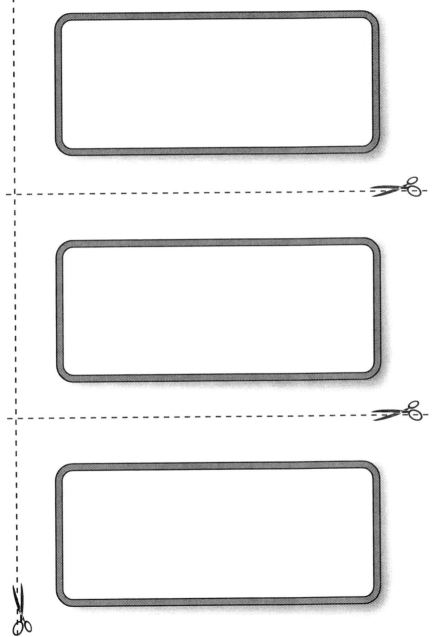

Correct Answers

Blank Cards for *Your Own Questions*

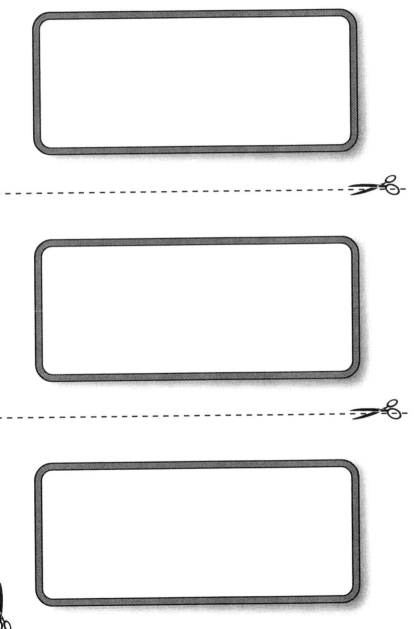

Correct Answers

Blank Cards for
Your Own Questions

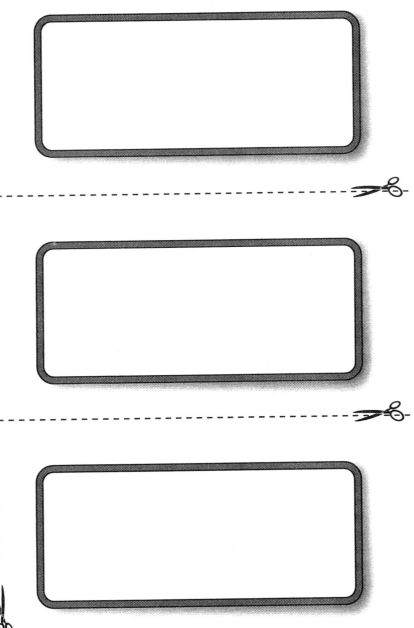

Correct Answers

Blank Cards for
Your Own Questions

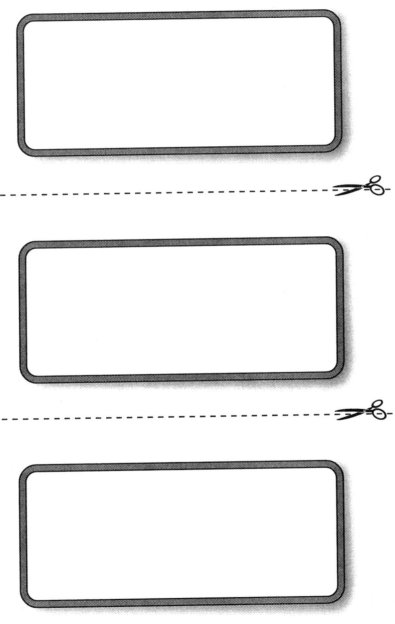

Correct Answers

Blank Cards for *Your Own Questions*

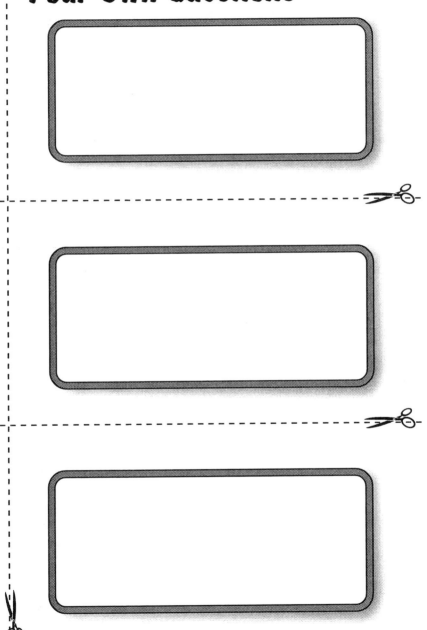

Correct Answers

INDEX

Adams, Sherman
   Resignation of 503
Adamson Act 1916 391
Agnew, Spiro
   Resignation of 268
Agricultural Adjustment Act 1933 442
Alliance for Progress
   Created 225
   Purpose of 225
Allied Control Council
   Governed by 169
America First Committee
   Aim of 126
American Association of Retired Persons (AARP) 564
American Liberty League
   Formed 444
   Objective of 444
   Supporters of 444
American Neutrality Patrol
   Purpose of 129
American Population 1930 422
Americans with Disabilities Act 1990 330
Anti-War Movement
   Factions 524
   Student Protest 1960s 523
Area Redevelopment Act of 1961 219
Atlantic Charter
   Purpose of 130
Atomic Bomb
   First detonated
      place 152
      time 152
   Manhattan Project 151
Atomic Energy Act of 1954
   Result of 199
Atomic Energy Commission
   Created 186
   Purpose of 186
Auto Immune Deficiency Syndrome (AIDS)
   Discovered 354
   Initial Victims
Bakker, Jim 577
Bankhead-Jones Farm Tenancy Act 1937
   Result 453
Banking Act 1933 84
Banking Act of 1935
   Purpose of 101
Baseball Player's Strike 1994
   Results of 385
Bay of Pigs Operation 223
Berlin Crisis 1948 485
   US response 485
Berlin Wall
   Erection of 515
   Fall of 339
Birth Control 526
Black Power Movement 1960s 522
Bonus Army
   Leader of 76
   Opposition to 76
Brady Bill 1993
   Provisions of 372
Bretton Woods Conference 167
Buchanan, Patrick
   Opposing Bush for Republican Nomination 1982 584
Budget and Accounting Act
   Affect on Federal Budget 61
Budget Reconciliation Act
   of 1981 295
   of 1993
      objective 368
Bull Moose Party
   Platform 1912 386
   Provisions of 386
Bush, George
   Administration's response to Soviet Union 320

Appointed "Drug Czar" 579
Arms control initiative 1991 576
Famous quotes of 318
Support in 1988 election 319
Supreme Court Appointees 332
Themes of 1988 Presidential
    Election 561
Cable Television Consumer
    Protection and Competition Act
    1992
        Results of 333
Camp David Accords 1978
    provisions of 281
Capone, Al 430
Carter, Jimmy
    Amnesty to Draft Dodgers
    541
    Criticism of Administration 277
    Foreign Policy 542
    Opposition to Democratic
        Nomination 1980 285
Ceausescu, Nicolae 567
Challenger Disaster 315
Child Labor Act
    Opposition to 12
    Significance of 12
China's declaration of Martial Law
    336
Civil Rights Act
    Of 1957
        purpose of 205
    Of 1964
        purpose of 229
    Of 1991
        results of 331
Civilian Conservation Corps (CCC)
    Eligibility in 88
    Work of 88
Clayton Antitrust Act
    Affect of 8
    Purpose of 8
Clear Air Act 1990
    Objective of 329
    Provisions of 329

Clinton, William Jefferson
    Campaign themes 1992 585
    Controversies of administration
    364
    Criticism of; for China's Most
        Favored Nation status 594
    "Gag Rule" lifted 587
    Health Care Reform 590
    Movement of Troops into
        Persian Gulf 1994 595
    Popular Vote won 1992 586
    Supreme Court appointees 374
    Whitewater Scandal 375
Commission of Base Realignment
    and Closure 1989 562
Commodity Credit Corporation
    Established 91
    Purpose of 91
Communism
    In China 170
        leader of 170
    In Czechoslovakia 165
    In Poland
        break away from 338
    Loss of monopoly in Soviet
        Union 350
Conciliation Treaties
    Exhibited 17
    Purpose of 17
Congressional economic
    legislation 1964 516
Congressional Elections
    Changes of 1980 544
    Republican Campaign themes
        591
    Significance of 1994 376
Congressional response to *Reuben
    James* 470
Constitution
    Nineteenth Amendment 40
    Sixteenth Amendment 6
    Twenty-first Amendment 81
    Twenty-second Amendment 191

Coolidge, Calvin
   Memorable quotes 65
Corporate Culture
   Critique of 212
   Significance of 204
Council on National Defense
   Chairpersons of 463
   Purpose of 463
Counter-culture & the New Left 240
"Court Packing" proposal
   Creation of 105
Crack Cocaine 355
Crime Bill 1994
   Authorized 373
Czechoslovakia
   Vaclav Havel 340
   life of 340
Dawes Plan
   Purpose of 69
Dean, John 537
Deb, Eugene
   Platform 1912 387
Declaration of United Nations 471
Deficit Reduction Act 1984 297
Democratic Party
   Nomination in 1956 502
   Nomination in 1984 303
   Opposition to Carter in 1980 285
   Platform in 1912 3
   Platform in 1932 77
   Platform in 1936 451
   Roosevelt re-elected 1940 128
   Split in 1948 192
"Détente" 264
Department of Housing and Urban Affairs 518
Disbanding of Soviet Union 352
   Replacement of 352
Dominican Republic
   Occurrence 1916 397

"Domino Theory" 245
Draft Abolished 257
Dukakis, Governor Michael
   Vice Presidential Running Mate Lloyd Bentsen 560
Eagleton, Senator Thomas
   Resignation as vice-presidential Nominee 1972 535
Economic Opportunity Act 1964
   Purpose of 230
Economic Recovery Act 1981 294
Eisenhower, Dwight D.
   Eisenhower Doctrine 178
   Legislative Program 500
   1958 Agreement with Krushchev 179
   Secretary of State 173
   Supreme Court Nominee 1953 200
Elementary and Secondary Education Act of 1965 232
Embargo on Japan 1940 467
Emergency Banking Relief Act 84
Emergency Fleet Corporation 1917
   Purpose of 407
Employment Act of 1964 185
   Purpose of 185
Equal Rights Amendment
   consequences of 288
Espionage and Sedition Acts 31
   Supreme Court involvement with 32
Exxon *Valdez* 325
Fair Deal Program
   Purpose of 193
Fair Employment Practice Committee
   Origins of 109
   Purpose of 109
Fair Labor Standards Act
   Terms for 107

Family Leave Act 1993 365
FDA response to effects of dietary fat 1994 599
Federal Farm Loan Act
    Purpose of 11, 90
Federal Highway Act
    Created 45
    Impact of 45
Federal Home Loan Bank Act 1932 438
Federal Reserve
    Attempt to stimulate economy 1991 324
    Federal Reserve Act passed 7
    Federal Reserve Notes, creation of 7
    Response to fears of inflation 1994 589
    Supervision of 7
Federal Trade Commission Act
    Purpose of 9
Federal Housing Administration (FHA)
    Purpose of 86
Federal Emergency Relief Act
    Administration of 87
    Purpose of 87
Fermi, Enrico 480
Flag Burning 327
Ford, Gerald
    Anti-Inflation Campaign 539
    Opposition to Republican Nomination 1976 276
Fordney McCumber Tariff
    Created 60
    Products affected 60
Foreign Policy
    Air strikes on Libya 554
    American troops in Lebanon consequence of 302
    Cuba 1960 184
    German invasion of USSR 131
    Intervention in Mexico 1916 20
    Invasion of Panama 1989 334
    Iraqi invasion of Kuwait 343
        commitment to Persian Gulf 344
    Japanese control of Indochina 132
    Manchurian Crisis 121
    Marines in Haiti 1915 396
        Wilson's justification 396
    Marines in Liberia 1990 337
    Opposition to Sandinista regime 552
    Outbreak of World War I 399
    Recognition of USSR 117
    Somalia 378
    Soviet invasion of Afghanistan 282
    Strategic missiles
        elimination of 307
    The People's Republic of China 279
    Troops sent to Haiti 1994 592
    US response to Chinese shelling of uemoy and Matsu 491
    USSR in the postwar era 162
Fourteen Points 34
Frazier-Lemke Farm Bankruptcy Act of 1934
    Purpose of 92
Freedom of Information Act
    Purpose of 271
"Freedom Riders" 221
Free Speech Movement
    On college campuses 238
Fuel Administration 405
Garner-Wagner Bill
    Hoover Veto 75
    Purpose of 75
Garvey, Marcus
    Ideology of 52

Gay Rights Movement 527
Geneva Accords
    Result of 176
    Role of US 176
General Maximum Price
    Regulation Act
        Established 137
        Purpose of 137
German reunification 566
GI Bill
    Purpose of 188
Good Neighbor Policy
    Purpose of 116
Gore-McLemore Resolution 400
    Results of 400
Great Depression
    Causes of 71
    Economics Effects of 72
    Reasons for Crash of 1929 71
Greater East Asia Co-Prosperity sphere 466
Grenada 1983 301
Gulf of Tonkin Resolution 243
    Purpose of 243
Guatemala
    Overthrow of President Guzman 182
Harding, Warren G.
    Secretary of State 431
    Teapot Dome scandal 62
Hart, Senator Gary
    Elimination from 1988 presidential race 559
Hawley-Smoot Tariff
    Created 73
    Problems with 73
Home ownership growth 1945-60 510
    Federal Housing Administration 512
Home Owners Loan Corporation 84

Hoover, Herbert
    Economic Philosophy 436
    "Hoovervilles" 437
    Support in 1932 78
Housing Act of 1961
    Provisions of 220
Hungary breaking from Communist bloc 565
Hydrogen Bomb
    Detonated 174
Illegitimate births 1980s 578
Immigration Act of 1965
    Effect of 233
Immigration Controversy 1917
    Congress' response to 393
    Important Consumer groups 1950s 511
Indian Reorganization Act
    Purpose of 110
Industry
    Use of assembly line 44
Iran-Contra Scandal 555
Iranian control of Embassy 1979 283
    Consequence of failed rescue attempt 284
Iraq
    Invasion of Kuwait 1990 justification of 342
Israeli - PLO accord 1994 379
Japanese Relocation Camps
    Elimination of 139
    Supreme Court decision on 139
    established 139
"Jazz Age"
    Characteristics of 51
Johnson Act of 1934
    Purpose of 118
Kellogg-Briand Pact
    Problems with 70
    Purpose of 70

Kennedy, John F.
  Assassination of 228
  Catholicism 508
  Margin of victory (popular vote) 1960 509
  National Guards sent to Mississippi 514
  Reaction of Soviet build-up in Cuba
    consequences of 226
    date 226
  Ordeals with Congress 218
Kennedy, Robert
  Assassination of 248
Kent State Riots 258
Kerner Commission
  On racial riots in 1960s 235
Kerr-McGillicuddy Act
  Impact of 13
Kevorkian, Dr. Jack 384
Khrushchev, Nikita
  1958 Agreement with Eisenhower 179
  Tour of US 180
King Jr., Martin Luther
  Assassinated by 236
Korean War
  Armistice 172
  McArthur 171
  Outcome 172
Ku Klux Klan decline 1925 429
Labor Movement
  Division of AFL and CIO 111
Labor Unions
  Drop in membership 1980s 356
Land-Lease
  Established 136
  Provisions 136
  Significance of 136
Landrum-Griffen Labor-Management Act
  Purpose of 202
Lansing Ishii Agreement 1917 394
League of Nations
  Opposition to 38
  US Senate and 39
    Wilson's influence 39
Levitt, William
  Housing Development 210
Lifted Economic Sanctions against Nicaragua 1990 335
Lithuanian declaration of independence 575
London Economic Conference
  Failure of 457
  1933 457
Los Angeles earthquake 1994 370
Los Angeles Riots 1991
  Losses of 359
  Precipitation of 359
Loyalty Review Board
  Creation of 195
  Purpose of 195
Lunar Landing 519
Malta Conference 1989 568
March on Washington 222
Marshall Plan
  objective of 164
Mayaguez Crisis of 1975 275
McCarren Internal Security Act
  Purpose of 196
  Truman opinion of 196
McCarthy, Eugene
  1968 presidential campaign issues 247
  Significance of New Hampshire primary 247
McCarthy, Senator Joseph 499
McGovern, George
  1972 presidential support 266
Medicare Act of 1965
  Purpose of 231

Median Age for Americans 1980 545
Medicare Catastrophic Coverage Act 1988
   Controversy of 328
"Me Generation" 290
Members of United Nations Security Council 487
Mondale, Walter
   Black American support in 1989 candidacy 553
   Support in 1984 election 304
Montevideo Conference 1933 456
"Moral Majority" 291
Motor Carrier Act 1935 450
"Motor-Voter" Bill 1993 367
Music Industry
   Reaction to 'indecency' attacks 358
Nation went off gold standard 84
National American Women Suffrage Association 392
National Commission of Excellence
   "A Nation at Risk" 361
   response to 362
National Defense Act 1916
   Purpose of 401
National Economy
   "Black Monday" 314
   Bonus Army 76
   Boston Police Strike 41
   Budget and Accounting Act 61
   Business Trends in 1920 47
   Cause of 1982 recession 548
   Coal Workers Strike 1919 414
      resolution of 414
   Consumer interest and demand 1920s 419
   Corporate Merger Phenomenon 313
   Decline of business loans 1920s 420
   Economic Slump of early 1970s 254
   Effect of Communist Revolution on 41
   Effect of Consumer Products 46
   Effects of postwar inflation 41
   Effects of Race Riots 1919
      causes of 42
      demographics 42
   Effect of Urbanization 50
   Federal Budget Deficit 1976 273
   Federal Budget Deficit 1983 296
   Financial Market scandal 1980s
      Lambert, Drexel Burnham 323
   Inflation rate in 1986 309
   Minimum Wage 1955 501
   Minimum Wage 1989 321
   New York City verge of bankruptcy 540
   Oil Prices
      affect of lowered prices on Banks 310
   Productivity from 1945-1955 207
   Reaction to threat of recession 1987 557
   Reasons for Boom of 1920s 417
   Recession of 1920
      factors of 416
   Rise in Farming Expenses 48
   Rural Poverty in 1966 234
   Savings and Loan problems 322
   Seattle General Strike 413
   Supply Side Economics 293
   Trade Deficits
      explanation of 312
   Unaffected sectors during late 1980s slowdown 563

Unemployment Rate 1993 600
Unionization of Mexican-
   American farm workers 237
Violent labor confrontations
   1920s 421
National Endowment for the Arts
   controversy 1989 582
National Industrial Recovery Act
   of 1934
      Purpose of 93
National Organization for Women
   (NOW)
      Founded 242
National Origin Act
   Purpose of 55
National Security Act of 1947
   Purpose of 190
National Service Act 1993 369
National Union for Social Justice
   leader 446
National Youth Administration 447
Nationalist Chinese government
   in Taiwan 488
Neutrality Acts
   1935, establishment of 119
   1936, 460
   1937, purpose of 120
   1939, 462
"New Federalism" 252
"New Freedom" 16
Nixon, Richard M.
   "Détente" 264
   Economic Initiatives of 1971 255
   Impeachment of Nixon 538
   Kissinger Meetings 262
   "New Federalism" 252
   1958 Latin American Tour 183
   Nominees to Supreme Court
      251, 531
   Pardon of 272
   Resignation of 269
   Running mate 1968 530
   Successor to 269

Watergate 267
   John Dean 537
   Welfare reform 532
Nobel Prize
   Toni Morrison 383
North American Free Trade
      Agreement (NAFTA) 371
   Prominent critics 371
North Atlantic Treaty Organization
(NATO)
   Formed 166
   Offer to former Warsaw Pact
      Members 1994 593
   Purpose of 166
North Korean invasion of South
   Korea 489
Nuclear Test Ban Treaty 224
Nye, Senator Gerald 459
OPEC 265
   Affect on US 265
Operation Rescue 580
Operation Rolling Thunder 244
Oklahoma City Bombing
   Suspects of 377
Organization Act 1949 496
Organized Crime
   Growth of 56
Panama Canal 395
Panama Canal Treaty
   Negotiated 278
   Provisions of 278
Paris Peace Conference 36
Parks, Rosa 507
Peace Corps
   Established 227
   Purpose 227
Pentagon Papers 259
Perkins, Frances 440
Persian Gulf War
   Alliances with Middle Eastern
      countries
         Egypt 569

I-8

Allied ground assault 347
   duration of 347
Casualties
   American 349
   Iraqi 349
Code name of 345
Commander of US forces 571
Congressional authorization 570
Instigation of 345
Permanent cease-fire established 573
Post-War Goals 574
SCUD Missile attacks
   primary targets 346
   purpose of 346
Terms of cease fire 348
Weapons commonly utilized 572
Political tendency of the "Sunbelt" 1980s 546
Popular Culture
   Cinema
      American Graffiti 547
      cinematic criticism of depression 114
      Lee, Spike 596
      movie attendance 53
      sound introduced 428
      Stone, Oliver 596
      The Crack in the Picture Window
         message of 215
      The Jazz Singer 428
      Vietnam War oriented 292
         Born on the Fourth of July 583
         Platoon 583
   Consumer Products
      Television 208
   Literature
      Death of a Salesman 216
      "Lost Generation" 54
      The "Beat" Writers 217
      The Feminine Mystique 241
      The Politics of Rich and Poor 581
   Music & Radio
      affect of 115
      "Jazz Age"
         Characteristics of 51
      Jazz & Blues 425
      Music Industry
         Reaction to 'indecency' attacks 358
      Swing & Big Band Music 455
   Society
      The "Me Generation" 290
   Travel
      Model T 418
Presidential Elections
   Election 1952
     results of 198
     significance of 198
   Election of 1960
     pivotal moments of 206
   Election of 1964 517
   Election of 1968
     results of 250
   Election of 1980
     results of 286
   Nominations 1912 4
   Nominations 1916 14
   Nominations 1920 43
   Nominations 1924 63
     results of 64
   Nominations 1988 317
   Perot, H. Ross
     significance of 363
   Progressive Party 63
   Smith, Alfred 67
   Socialist Party, popularity of 1
   World War I, effect on 23

Presidential Succession Act 1947 498
Progressive Party platform 1924 433
Prohibition
  Establishment of 412
Protestant Unity 1920s 427
Public Works Administration
  Objective of 89
  Operation of 89
Race Relations in Arkansas 1957 506
Reagan, Ronald
  Anti-Union Measures 550
  Assassination attempt on 298
  Criticism to appointed officials 300
  Farm Policy 311
  Grenada 301
  Inauguration and hostage release 287
  Supreme Court appointments 558
  Supreme Court Nominee 1986 316
  Terminology of Soviet Union 551
  Vice Presidential Nominee 1980 543
Reconstruction Finance Cooperation
  Purpose of 74
Religion
  Catholic Church controversies 598
  Church Population 1960 214
  Return to churches for "Baby Boomers" 597
Republican Party
  Nomination of 1912 2
  Nomination of 1936 452
  Nomination of 1949 474
  Opposition to Ford in 1976 276
  Platform in 1920 415
  Platform in 1924 432
Reserve Act
  of 1935 102
  of 1942 473
Resettlement Administration (RA) 448
Revenue Acts
  Act of 1918 408
  Act of 1926
    features of 66
  Purpose of 59
Roe v. Wade 289
Roosevelt, Franklin D.
  "Court Packing" proposal 105
  Death of 141
  Democratic Nomination 1932 439
  Democratic re-election in 1940 128
  First One Hundred Days 441
  Gubernatorial Positions 79
  Inaugural Slogan 82
  Legislation
    Legislation of 1933 84
    New Deal Coalition
      composition of 104
    The First New Deal 83
      criticism of 95
      effectiveness of 443
    The Second New Deal 96
  Reluctance to anti-lynching legislation 108
  Support in 1936 election 103
  Unofficial advisers 80
Roosevelt, Theodore
  Speeches of 461
    public response 461
  vice-presidents of 464

Rosenburg Case 197
Rural Electrification
   Administration (R.E.A.)
     Purpose of 98
Sacco & Vanzetti 58
SALT Treaty of 1972 263
SALT II
   Consequences of 280
Sandinistas and Contras cease-fire 556
Sandino, General Augusto 435
Scopes Trial
   Focus of 57
Second Agricultural Adjustment Act 1938 454
Securities and Exchange Commission (SEC)
   Purpose of 85
Selective Services Act 25
Selective Service and Training Act
   Objective of 127
Sexual Revolution
   Affect on women's clothing 1920 424
Share Our Wealth Society 1934 445
Smith Act of 1940
   Purpose of 194
   Use of 194
Smith, Alfred
   Significance of 67
Smith-Connolly Act
   Purpose of 138
Smith-Hughes Act 1917 426
Smith v. Millwright
   Importance of 140
Social Security Act
   Provisions of 100
Southeast Asia Treaty Organization 490
   Members of 490

Soviet Annexation of Poland, Hungary, Rumania, and Bulgaria 484
Soviet testing of atomic weapons 486
Space Exploration
   Challenger Disaster 315
   Sputnik 201
   consequences 201
START Treaty 1990
   Accomplishments of 341
START II Treaty 1993
   Results of 353
Strategic Defense Initiative (SDI; Star Wars) 306
   Fate of 306
Stevenson, Alan
   Support in 1956 502
Students for a Democratic Society (SDS) 239
Submarine Crisis 1915 21
Suburban Growth 49
Suez Canal Crisis
   Date of 177
   Significance of 177
Suffrage Amendment
   Defeated by 409
Summit Conference 1955
   Members of 492
   Purpose of 492
Sun Belt
   Growth in Population 209
Supply Side Economics 293
Supreme Court
   Ada Lois Sipuel v. Board of Regents 504
   Brandeis, Louis 10
   Brown v. Board of Education 204
   First Women appointed to 299

I-11

Korematsu v. United States 139
Roe v. Wade 289
Smith v. Millwright decision 140
Sweatt v. Painter 504
Webster v. Reproductive Health Services 357
Sussex Pledge 22
Taft-Hartley Act
    Affect on Unions 189
Tailhook Scandal 1991 360
Tax Equity and Fiscal
    Responsibility Act 549
Tax Reform Act 1986
    Provisions of 308
Tennessee Valley Authority (T.V.A.)
    Purpose of 94
    Represented 94
Trade Embargo Lifted on Vietnam 1994 381
Truman, Harry S.
    Civil Rights measures enacted 497
    Gubernatorial experience 493
    1946 Railway Strike 187
    Price Control elimination 494
        exemptions to 494
Truth-in Securities Act 84
Tydings-McDuffie Act 1934 458
U-2 Incident 181
Underwood-Simmons Tariff Act 1913
    Accomplishments of 390
Unions
    Members
        1941 113
    United Mine Workers
        Lewis, John L. 112
Union of the Soviet Socialist Republic (USSR)
    Characteristics of
        Gorbachev's regime 305
        Election freedom 350
        Leaders of 175, 305
        Military Coup 1991 351
United Mine Workers
    Leader of 495
United Nations
    Established 168
Urban Areas most populated 423
US - Cuban immigration agreement 1994 382
US-Japanese summit conference 1941 468
US - North Korea agreement 1994 380
US Occupation of Iceland 465
US Railroad Administration
    Action of 406
US States
    Alaska 203
    Hawaii 203
US Virgin Islands
    Acquired from 398
    Date 398
Versailles Treaty 37
Veteran's endowment 1924 434
Vietnam War
    American presence 528
    Congressional investigations 1966 529
    Continued Bombing 1972 534
    Exodus from Vietnam 261
    My Lai 533
    Peace Treaty
        conditions of 260
    The Fall of Saigon 274
    The Tet Offensive 246
    "Vietnamization" 256
Voting Age Lowered to 18 253
Voting Rights Act of 1965 520
Waco Crisis 1993 588
Wagner Act
    Enactment of 99
    Purpose of 99

Wagner-Steagall Act
   Enactment of 106
   Purpose of 106
Wallace, Governor George
   Appeal in 1968 presidential election 249
   Assassination attempt 536
War Industries Board 28
War Labor Board 29
   W.W.I affect on 29
War Powers Act of 1973 270
War Production Board 472
War Resources Board
   Establishment 125
   Purpose 125
Washington Conference
   Treaties of 68
Watergate 267
Watts Riots 1965
   Casualties 521
Wheeler-Rayburn Act 1935 449
White Citizens Council 505
"White Flight" 211
Wilson, Woodrow 3
   Bryan-Chamosso treaty 19
   Dollar diplomacy, opposition to 18
   Fourteen Points
      message of 34
   Gubernatorial Positions 5
   Legislative Promise 1913
      features of 389
   "New Freedom" 16
   1918 Congressional Elections 35
   Paris Peace Conference 36
   Popular vote 1916 15
   Secretary of State 388
Women
   Movement 525
   Roles after W.W.II 213

Works Progress Administration (W.P.A.)
   Operation of 97
Work Week 1950s 513
World Trade Center Bombing 1993
   Convictions of
World War One
   Affect on Prohibition 410
   American declaration of War 24
      on Germany 402
   Armistice of 27
   Causes of
      Submarine Crisis 1915 21
   Commanders of
      Pershing 26
   Effect on Minorities 33
   Military Engagements 404
   Public Mood 30
   Role of Blacks 403
   Selective Services Act 25
   Versailles Treaty
      German defiance to 123
      provisions of 37
   Versailles Conference
      affect of Bolshevik Revolution on 411
World War Two
   Allied Invasion of Italy 143
      Fall of Rome 143
   Allied Invasion of North Africa 475
      General Erwin Rommel's surrender 476
   Allied liberation of Paris 477
   Attack on Hiroshima 153
      Casualties of 153
   Attack on Nagasaki 483
   Battle of the Bulge
      origin of 145
      date of 145

Battle of the Coral Sea 146
    significance of 146
Battle of Midway 147
    importance of 147
Battle of the Philippine Sea
    result in Japan 148
Battle of Okinawa
    significance of 150
Casablanca Conference 155
    significance of 155
D-Day
    significance of 144
Declaration of Cairo
    issued 157
    purpose of 157
German Invasion of Soviet Union 469
German surrender 478
"Iron Curtain" Speech
    Place 161
Italian invasion of Ethiopia 122
Japanese Surrender 154
Liberation of Manila 479
Kamikaze attacks 149
    date of first use 149
Moscow Conference 156
Pearl Harbor
    alternate attack site 133
    Casualties 134
    Kassarine Pass
        outcome 142
    Roosevelt's response 135
Origins 124
Potsdam Conference 160
    Date 160
Soviet entrance against Japan 482
Teheran Conference 158
    Date 158
The Enola Gay 481
Yalta Conference
    Soviet Agreement to 159
Wright, Jim
    resignation 1989 326